Unlocking Home Equity

The Ultimate Guide to Reverse Mortgage

By Gian Carlo Bavaro

GIAN CARLO BAVARO, MBA

RESIDENTIAL MORTGAGE & REVERSE MORTGAGE SPECIALIST

- 📞 (954) 228-0828
- ✉ Gian@ReverseMortgageSouthFlorida.com
- 🌐 www.ReverseMortgageSouthFlorida.com
- 🏠 NMLS #1502605
- 🗣 Se Habla Español

Corporate NMLS# 1700825 — 221 W Hallandale Beach Blvd #101, Hallandale Beach, FL 33009

Copyright © 2024 Gian Carlo Bavaro

All rights reserved.

About Gian Carlo Bavaro

Gian Carlo Bavaro is a trusted expert in the reverse mortgage field, dedicated to serving the unique needs of homeowners in South Florida. As the founder and owner of ReverseMortgageSouthFlorida.com and the head of the reverse mortgage division at his current company, Gian brings years of specialized experience, integrity, and an unwavering commitment to helping clients make informed, confident financial decisions. His journey in the mortgage industry began in 2016, building on a solid academic foundation: he graduated top of his class at Florida Atlantic University in 2011 and went on to complete an accelerated international MBA program at Florida International University (FIU) in 2012. Since then, Gian has originated over 500 residential loans, earning a reputation for excellence and honesty, and establishing himself as a top-rated mortgage professional online.

Deeply rooted in his South Florida community, Gian is a proud resident of Coconut Creek and a devoted member of Calvary Chapel Fort Lauderdale, where he has attended since 2010. In 2024, he was licensed as a minister through Christian Leaders Alliance, allowing him to further serve in both the men's discipleship and business ministries at his church. With a focus on integrity and servant leadership, he dedicates time to supporting those around him through mentorship and spiritual guidance.

Beyond his professional and ministry roles, Gian values time with his family. He and his wife, Janae, have been happily married for over a decade and are the proud parents of three young sons. A South Florida native, born and raised in Broward County, Gian has a passion for local culture and community. In his free time, he enjoys family cruises, reading about history and finance, playing chess, and casual PC gaming.

Fully bilingual in English and Spanish, Gian is proud to connect with clients across diverse backgrounds. Through his honesty, integrity, and deep knowledge of reverse mortgages, Gian Carlo Bavaro continues to make a positive impact on the lives of those he serves in the vibrant South Florida community.

Contents

1	Understanding Reverse Mortgages: The Basics	1
2	Key Factors That Influence Eligibility	4
3	When a Reverse Mortgage May Not Be the Best Choice	9
4	Leveraging Reverse Mortgages for Long-Term Care	13
5	Loan Structure and Limits	17
6	Understanding Non-Recourse and Financial Protections	21
7	The Homeowner's Financial Responsibilities	25
8	Special Loan Features: Line of Credit and Growth	30
9	Understanding Loan Options: Fixed vs. Adjustable Rates	35
10	Payout Structures and Locking in Your Interest Rate	40
11	What Happens to the Home After Death	45
12	Reverse Mortgage Costs Explained	49
13	Protecting the Borrower: Counseling and Non-Borrowing Spouse	54
14	HECM and Refinancing Options	59
15	Advanced Planning and Tax Considerations	64
16	Government Benefits and Equity Impact	69
17	Reverse Mortgage and Retirement Planning: Strategic Timing for Maximum Benefit	74
18	Proprietary Reverse Mortgages and Loan Servicing	79
19	Paying Off a Reverse Mortgage and Helpful Hints	85
20	Next Steps and Ideal Candidates	90

CHAPTER 1

UNDERSTANDING REVERSE MORTGAGES: THE BASICS

Reverse mortgages can be a valuable financial tool for homeowners nearing or in retirement, but they are often misunderstood. In this chapter, we will break down what a reverse mortgage is, how it works, and the benefits and risks associated with this type of loan.

What Is a Reverse Mortgage?

At its core, a reverse mortgage is a type of loan available to homeowners who are typically 62 years or older. Unlike traditional mortgages, where the borrower makes monthly payments to the lender, a reverse mortgage works in reverse: the lender makes payments to the homeowner. The amount of the loan is based on factors such as the home's value, the homeowner's age, and current interest rates.

The most common reverse mortgage is the Home Equity Conversion Mortgage (HECM), which is insured by the Federal Housing Administration (FHA). This ensures that even if the loan balance exceeds the value of the home, neither the borrower nor their heirs will owe more than the home is worth when the loan becomes due.

How Does It Work?

When you take out a reverse mortgage, you are essentially borrowing against the equity in your home. You can receive these funds in several ways: as a lump sum, monthly payments, a line of credit, or a combination of these options. The loan balance increases over time as interest accrues, but no payments are required as long as you continue to live in the home, keep it in good condition, and meet all required obligations like property taxes and insurance.

The loan only becomes due when one of several "maturity events" occurs, which can include selling the home, moving out permanently, or the borrower passing away.

Who Can Benefit from a Reverse Mortgage?

Reverse mortgages are designed for older homeowners who want to access the equity in their homes to fund their retirement. They can be particularly helpful for individuals who have significant equity but may not have enough liquid savings or income to meet their financial needs. The funds from a reverse mortgage can be used for various purposes, such as supplementing retirement income, paying off medical bills, covering living expenses, or even funding home renovations.

The Benefits of a Reverse Mortgage

- No Monthly Mortgage Payments: Perhaps the biggest draw is that you are not required to make monthly mortgage payments. Instead, the loan balance grows over time, and repayment is deferred until the loan matures.
- Access to Tax-Free Funds: The money you receive from a reverse mortgage is generally not considered taxable income, which can help stretch your retirement savings.
- Flexible Disbursement Options: Borrowers can choose how they wish to receive their funds—whether it's a lump sum, regular payments, or access to a line of credit.
- FHA Insurance Protection: Because most reverse mortgages are insured by the FHA, you are protected against the possibility of owing more than the home is worth when it's time to repay the loan.

Things to Keep in Mind

While reverse mortgages can be beneficial, they are not for everyone. It's important to consider the following:

- The Loan Balance Increases Over Time: Since you are not making payments, the loan balance will grow as interest is added to the amount you owe. This can reduce the equity in your home.
- Homeowner Responsibilities Remain: You are still responsible for paying property taxes, homeowners insurance, and keeping the home in good condition. Failure to do so can result in the loan becoming due.
- Impact on Inheritance: Reverse mortgages can reduce the value of your estate, leaving less for your heirs. However, if you're not concerned about leaving behind an inheritance or if your home is no longer a primary asset, this may not be a significant drawback.

Is a Reverse Mortgage Right for You?

A reverse mortgage may be the right choice if you're seeking to access your home's equity without the burden of monthly payments, especially if you plan to stay in your home for the long term. However, it's important to evaluate your overall financial situation and goals. For some, downsizing or selling the home outright might make more sense.

In the chapters ahead, we will dive deeper into the specifics of reverse mortgages, from eligibility requirements and obligations to interest rates and payout options. This chapter is only the beginning, but it provides a foundation to understand the key components of reverse mortgages and how they may fit into your financial plan.

CHAPTER 2

KEY FACTORS THAT INFLUENCE ELIGIBILITY

While reverse mortgages offer a unique way for homeowners to unlock the equity in their homes, not everyone qualifies. This chapter will guide you through the main eligibility criteria for obtaining a reverse mortgage, ensuring you understand the requirements and whether this option aligns with your financial needs.

1. Age Requirement

The most fundamental requirement for a reverse mortgage is the age of the borrower. For the Home Equity Conversion Mortgage (HECM)—the most common type of reverse mortgage insured by the FHA—you must be at least 62 years old. If you are applying as a couple, only one borrower needs to meet this age requirement, but the terms of the loan may vary depending on the age and status of the younger spouse.

Why Age Matters:

The amount of money you can borrow depends on your age—the older you are, the more equity you can unlock. Lenders factor in age because the loan balance accumulates over time, and older borrowers are expected to accrue less interest before the loan becomes due.

2. Home Equity and Property Type

To qualify for a reverse mortgage, you must have significant equity in your home—generally at least 50%. The more equity you have, the more you'll be able to borrow. Homes with little to no equity are not eligible for a reverse mortgage, and borrowers must own their home outright or have a low remaining balance on any existing mortgages, which will need to be paid off as part of the reverse mortgage.

Eligible property types include:
- Single-family homes
- 2- to 4-unit properties (as long as the borrower occupies one of the units)
- FHA-approved condominiums
- Some manufactured homes (must meet FHA guidelines)

Why Home Equity Matters:

Your home serves as collateral for the loan, so lenders need to ensure there's enough value in the property to cover the loan balance, including interest over time.

3. Primary Residence Requirement

To obtain a reverse mortgage, your home must be your primary residence, meaning you live in the property for the majority of the year. Vacation homes and investment properties are not eligible for reverse mortgages under the HECM program.

You will be required to certify that the home remains your primary residence every year. Moving out of the home for more than 12 consecutive months, whether due to health issues or other reasons, can trigger the loan to become due.

4. Home Maintenance and Condition

The lender will conduct an appraisal to ensure the home is in good condition. Major repairs or maintenance issues can disqualify a property from eligibility or delay the approval process. In some cases, a portion of the reverse mortgage proceeds may be set aside to cover necessary repairs before the loan is finalized.

Why Home Condition Matters:
The home serves as collateral for the loan, so lenders need to ensure it remains in good condition to preserve its value. Homeowners are responsible for maintaining the property, and failure to do so could result in the loan becoming due.

5. Financial Obligations: Taxes, Insurance, and HOA Dues

As a reverse mortgage borrower, you must remain current on property taxes, homeowners insurance, and any homeowners association (HOA) fees. If you fall behind on these obligations, it can result in the loan being called due and payable.

Before approving your loan, the lender will conduct a financial assessment to ensure you have the means to cover these ongoing expenses. If they determine that you may struggle with these costs, they may require a Life Expectancy Set-Aside (LESA), where a portion of your loan proceeds is reserved to pay these expenses on your behalf.

Why Financial Obligations Matter:
Even though reverse mortgages don't require monthly loan payments, you are still responsible for maintaining the financial responsibilities tied to the home. Falling behind on taxes or insurance could lead to foreclosure, which is why lenders are diligent in assessing your ability to meet these obligations.

6. Counseling Requirement

Before you can finalize a reverse mortgage, you must participate in a counseling session with a HUD-approved counselor. This requirement ensures that you fully understand the reverse mortgage process, costs, and obligations, and it provides an opportunity to ask questions and explore alternatives.

Counseling sessions are often conducted over the phone and are designed to give you a clear picture of how a reverse mortgage will impact your financial situation.

Why Counseling Matters:
Reverse mortgages are complex financial products, and counseling ensures that you make an informed decision. It is an essential safeguard to help protect seniors from misunderstandings or entering into a loan that may not suit their needs.

7. Credit and Income Review

While reverse mortgages are not based on credit scores or income levels the way traditional loans are, lenders still conduct a review to determine if the borrower can meet the ongoing costs of property ownership, such as taxes, insurance, and maintenance. Poor credit or insufficient income may result in a lender requiring set-asides to cover these costs. However, poor credit alone is not a reason for loan denial.

Why Credit and Income Matter:

The lender's primary concern is that you will be able to stay current on your financial obligations related to the home, preventing any risk of default. While reverse mortgages offer flexibility, lenders want to ensure you can comfortably sustain homeownership throughout the life of the loan.

CHAPTER 3

WHEN A REVERSE MORTGAGE MAY NOT BE THE BEST CHOICE

Reverse mortgages can provide a flexible financial solution for older homeowners, but they aren't the right option for everyone. Understanding when a reverse mortgage might not be in your best interest is crucial for making a sound financial decision. In this chapter, we will explore situations where taking out a reverse mortgage could create more challenges than benefits.

1. Short-Term Living Plans

If you are considering moving or selling your home within a few years, a reverse mortgage may not be the best option. Reverse mortgages are designed to work over the long term, and the initial costs associated with setting up the loan can be high. These include origination fees, mortgage insurance premiums, and closing costs. If you plan to move in the near future, the costs of establishing a reverse mortgage may outweigh the benefits, as you will be required to repay the loan as soon as you sell or vacate the home.

Better Alternatives:
In this case, selling your home or downsizing might provide you with more immediate liquidity without the upfront expenses of a reverse mortgage.

2. Wanting to Leave a Significant Inheritance

For homeowners who want to leave their property as a substantial part of their estate, a reverse mortgage may not be the ideal choice. Since reverse mortgages accrue interest and fees over time, the balance owed will increase, which reduces the amount of equity left in the home. Depending on the length of the loan and market conditions, this can significantly reduce the inheritance you leave to your heirs.

Better Alternatives:
If preserving home equity for your heirs is a priority, you may want to consider other financial options, such as home equity loans or lines of credit, which allow you to tap into your home's value while maintaining more control over the amount owed.

3. Struggling with Ongoing Homeownership Costs

Reverse mortgages do not relieve homeowners of all financial responsibilities. You will still need to cover property taxes, homeowners insurance, and any necessary maintenance or repairs. If you are currently struggling to manage these costs, a reverse mortgage may only provide temporary relief. Falling behind on these obligations can lead to default, which may result in foreclosure.

Better Alternatives:
If maintaining the home has become a financial burden, selling the property and downsizing to a more affordable option might make more sense. This can free up funds and reduce the ongoing costs associated with homeownership.

4. You Are Not Ready to Commit to a Complex Financial Product

Reverse mortgages are complex financial products with various terms and conditions that can be difficult to understand. If you're not fully comfortable with the loan structure or don't fully grasp the long-term implications, it might be better to wait until you have a clearer understanding. Counseling sessions are required for a reason—reverse mortgages require careful thought and planning, especially since they impact your financial future and estate.

Better Alternatives:
Before committing to a reverse mortgage, consider speaking with a financial advisor or exploring other retirement income strategies that you might find easier to understand and manage.

5. Your Health May Require You to Move Soon

If you or your spouse are experiencing health issues that could require long-term care or relocation to an assisted living facility, a reverse mortgage could become problematic. The loan becomes due if you no longer occupy the home as your primary residence for more than 12 consecutive months. This means that if you need to move into a care facility, the reverse mortgage balance must be repaid, which may force the sale of your home at a time when you're least prepared for it.

Better Alternatives:
In cases where health is a concern, it may be better to explore alternative financial strategies, such as selling your home and using the proceeds to pay for long-term care.

6. You're Not Sure About Sharing Financial Decisions with a Lender

With a reverse mortgage, your home becomes collateral for the loan, and the lender has a vested interest in ensuring it is properly maintained. You may be required to set aside funds for repairs or other obligations if the lender deems it necessary. This additional oversight can feel restrictive, especially if you prefer to have full control over your finances and property.

Better Alternatives:
If you are uncomfortable with sharing decision-making power with a lender, a traditional home equity loan or line of credit might provide more autonomy while still allowing you to access your home's value.

7. Your Spouse Is Not 62 or Older

If you have a spouse who is not yet 62, you may want to reconsider a reverse mortgage or explore other options. While some protections exist for non-borrowing spouses, such as allowing them to remain in the home after the borrowing spouse passes away, there are potential risks. For example, if your non-borrowing spouse does not qualify to remain on the title, they could be required to leave the home if the borrowing spouse dies or moves into long-term care.

Better Alternatives:
It's essential to carefully review the protections in place for non-borrowing spouses and consider other financial products that won't jeopardize your spouse's ability to remain in the home.

Conclusion

While reverse mortgages can be a powerful tool for certain homeowners, they are not a one-size-fits-all solution. If any of the above scenarios apply to you, it may be worth reconsidering whether a reverse mortgage is the best option for your financial situation. Understanding the potential drawbacks and carefully weighing your options can help you avoid making a decision that could lead to future financial strain.

CHAPTER 4

LEVERAGING REVERSE MORTGAGES FOR LONG-TERM CARE

As seniors age, healthcare costs often become a significant concern, particularly when it comes to long-term care. One of the less discussed but highly effective uses of a reverse mortgage is to provide funding for these expenses, allowing homeowners to tap into their home equity to cover costs without having to sell or move out of their home. This chapter will explore how reverse mortgages can be strategically leveraged to meet the growing demand for long-term care, including in-home care, medical expenses, or even assisted living.

1. Using Reverse Mortgages for In-Home Care

For many seniors, the preference is to remain in their homes for as long as possible, a concept often referred to as "aging in place." However, this can sometimes require hiring in-home care services, which may include help with daily living activities, home modifications, or medical equipment. In these cases, reverse mortgage proceeds can provide the necessary financial flexibility to pay for in-home care while allowing the homeowner to remain in the comfort of their home.

How It Works:

Homeowners can opt to receive their reverse mortgage proceeds in monthly payments or as a line of credit, giving them the flexibility to cover care-related costs as they arise.

This can include paying for caregivers, home health aides, physical therapists, and other professionals who support aging in place.

Key Benefits:

By using a reverse mortgage for in-home care, seniors can avoid selling their home to fund their care needs. Additionally, they retain ownership and continue living in their familiar environment, which can contribute to improved quality of life.

2. Covering Medical and Healthcare Expenses

The cost of healthcare often increases as we age, with expenses like medications, doctor visits, surgeries, and specialized treatments becoming more frequent. These costs can quickly overwhelm traditional retirement savings or fixed incomes. A reverse mortgage can serve as a source of funds to cover medical bills, allowing homeowners to manage healthcare expenses without having to dip into savings or sell investments.

Using Proceeds for Healthcare:

Reverse mortgage funds can be used to pay for various medical expenses, including long-term prescriptions, hospital stays, and ongoing therapies. Homeowners can choose a lump sum payment option to cover larger expenses, like surgeries or medical emergencies, or they can use monthly payments to cover regular, smaller healthcare costs.

Medicare and Medicaid Considerations:

While Medicare covers many healthcare costs, it doesn't cover everything—especially long-term care. Reverse mortgage proceeds can help bridge the gap for out-of-pocket medical expenses not covered by Medicare or private insurance. However, for those receiving Medicaid, it's important to manage reverse mortgage proceeds carefully to avoid affecting eligibility.

3. Funding Assisted Living or Nursing Home Care

In some cases, staying at home may no longer be an option due to health reasons, requiring seniors to move into assisted living facilities or nursing homes. Reverse mortgages can be used to fund these living arrangements, provided the borrower maintains their home as a primary residence or plans for it to be sold when they move into care.

Using the Funds for Assisted Living:

While a reverse mortgage cannot be kept indefinitely if the borrower moves permanently into an assisted living facility or nursing home, it can still serve as a short-term solution to cover these expenses. Borrowers can use the proceeds to pay for the initial costs of moving into assisted living, including deposits and monthly fees.

Home Sale Option:

Another option is for the home to be sold after the borrower moves into care, with the proceeds from the sale used to repay the reverse mortgage and any remaining funds directed toward long-term care expenses. This can be a helpful strategy for seniors who need to transition out of their home but don't have other liquid assets to cover the costs of long-term care facilities.

4. Modifying the Home for Aging in Place

For seniors who wish to remain at home but need modifications to make their environment safer and more accessible, reverse mortgages can provide the necessary funds for home renovations. Common modifications include installing ramps, widening doorways, adding grab bars in bathrooms, and upgrading lighting.

Home Renovation with Reverse Mortgage Funds:

Borrowers can use a lump sum or line of credit to pay for these renovations, helping to ensure the home is better suited to meet their physical needs as they age. Modifying the home for accessibility not only improves safety but can also prevent accidents that might otherwise necessitate a move into assisted living.

Improved Quality of Life:

By making these modifications, seniors can continue living in a comfortable, familiar environment while minimizing the risk of injury or falls. This can lead to a higher quality of life and prolong the ability to live independently.

5. Planning for Future Long-Term Care Needs

One of the major advantages of reverse mortgages is their flexibility. Borrowers can choose to set up a line of credit that grows over time, giving them access to funds when they need them most. This is particularly useful for long-term care planning, where expenses might not be immediate but could arise later.

Growth of Line of Credit:

If the borrower sets up a line of credit, any unused funds will grow over time. This means that by establishing a reverse mortgage early in retirement, borrowers can create a financial safety net that increases in value as they age. When care needs arise, they can draw from this line of credit to cover medical or long-term care costs.

Tax-Free Proceeds:

The money accessed from a reverse mortgage is not considered taxable income, meaning that seniors can use these funds without worrying about how it will affect their tax liability. This can be particularly useful for retirees who are managing other income sources, such as Social Security or pension plans.

Conclusion

For seniors facing the growing costs of long-term care, a reverse mortgage can provide a powerful tool to access home equity without selling the home or taking on additional debt payments. Whether used for in-home care, medical expenses, assisted living, or home modifications, reverse mortgage proceeds offer financial flexibility for aging homeowners. By strategically leveraging their home's value, seniors can maintain a higher quality of life and ensure they have the resources to meet their long-term care needs.

CHAPTER 5: LOAN STRUCTURE AND LIMITS

Understanding how reverse mortgage loan limits and structures work is crucial to making informed decisions about your financial future. This chapter covers the essential details of how much you can borrow, how that amount is determined, and the key events that could cause the loan to become due.

1. Initial Disbursement Limits

When you first take out a reverse mortgage, especially under the Home Equity Conversion Mortgage (HECM) program, there are rules governing how much of your loan proceeds you can access immediately. This is referred to as the initial disbursement limit.

For the first year, HECM loans limit the amount you can borrow based on two main factors:

- Your available principal limit (determined by age, home value, interest rates, and FHA loan limits)

- How much is needed to pay off any existing mortgages or liens

If you need to use the reverse mortgage to pay off a significant existing loan balance, you may not have immediate access to much of the remaining loan proceeds during the first 12 months. The remaining funds will be available after the first year.

Why Initial Limits Exist:

The limits on initial disbursements help protect both borrowers and lenders from depleting the available loan proceeds too quickly. These limits are in place to ensure there are sufficient funds available over the long term to cover loan costs and potential future needs.

2. Principal Limit: How Much Can You Borrow?

The principal limit is the maximum amount you can borrow with a reverse mortgage. This limit is calculated using a variety of factors:

- The borrower's age: Older borrowers generally have access to a higher principal limit because their life expectancy is shorter, meaning the loan is expected to accumulate less interest over time.

- The home's appraised value: Higher-valued homes can access more loan proceeds.

- Current interest rates: Lower interest rates increase the amount you can borrow, while higher rates reduce it.

- FHA loan limits: For HECM loans, there are maximum limits on how much you can borrow, regardless of your home's value.

Here's how each factor affects the loan:

- Age: The older you are when you take out the loan, the more you can borrow. For example, a 75-year-old will typically be able to borrow more than a 62-year-old because the loan is expected to accrue interest for a shorter period.

- Interest Rates: Lower rates allow borrowers to unlock more of their home's equity. Higher interest rates reduce the available funds because more of the loan proceeds will go toward covering interest over time.

- Home Value: The more your home is worth, the more equity you can potentially access. However, FHA-imposed loan limits cap the maximum loan amount, so if your home's value exceeds the limit, you may not be able to access all of its equity through a HECM loan.

3. What Happens if You Max Out Your Principal Limit?

It's possible that, over time, you could max out your available principal limit. As interest accrues and draws are made, the loan balance grows, eating into your available equity. Once you reach your principal limit, you will no longer be able to take additional draws from the reverse mortgage.

However, even if you max out the principal limit, you will not owe more than the value of your home due to the non-recourse feature of HECM loans, which we'll discuss further in the next chapter.

4. Maturity Events: When Is the Loan Due?

Reverse mortgages differ from traditional loans because they do not require monthly mortgage payments. However, certain events can trigger the loan to become due, referred to as maturity events. These include:

- Selling the home: If you sell your home, the reverse mortgage becomes due. The loan balance will be paid from the proceeds of the sale, and any remaining equity is yours.

- Moving out permanently: If the home is no longer your primary residence, whether because you've moved into long-term care or relocated elsewhere, the loan will come due. In this case, you or your heirs may sell the home or refinance to repay the loan.

- Borrower passes away: After the death of the borrower (or the last surviving borrower in the case of co-borrowers), the loan becomes due. Heirs have the option to repay the loan, usually by selling the home or paying off the balance with other funds. If the home is worth less than the loan balance, the non-recourse feature protects heirs from owing more than the home's appraised value.

- Failure to meet ongoing obligations: As the homeowner, you are required to continue paying property taxes, homeowners insurance, and other obligations like HOA fees. If you fail to keep up with these payments, or if the home falls into disrepair, the lender may declare the loan due.

Why Maturity Events Matter:

Knowing the triggers that cause the loan to become due helps you prepare for the future. Whether you're planning to stay in your home for the long term or considering a move, understanding these maturity events ensures you aren't caught off guard by the loan repayment requirements.

5. Repayment and What Happens Next

Once a maturity event occurs, the loan will need to be repaid. In most cases, the home is sold to cover the balance of the loan. Any remaining equity after the loan is repaid belongs to the homeowner or their heirs. If the sale doesn't cover the full balance of the loan, the non-recourse nature of the loan ensures that neither you nor your heirs will owe more than the value of the home.

If your heirs wish to keep the home, they can repay the loan balance themselves, either with savings or by refinancing the home.

Conclusion

Understanding the loan structure and limits of a reverse mortgage is crucial for making informed decisions about your financial future. From initial disbursement limits to principal limit calculations, each aspect affects how much money you can access and how long the funds will last. Moreover, knowing the maturity events that trigger repayment will help you and your family prepare for the future, ensuring that you maintain control over your home and finances.

In the next chapter, we will explore the protections in place for borrowers, including the non-recourse feature and the financial safety nets built into the reverse mortgage structure.

CHAPTER 6

UNDERSTANDING NON-RECOURSE AND FINANCIAL PROTECTIONS

One of the key advantages of reverse mortgages, particularly the federally-insured Home Equity Conversion Mortgage (HECM), is the suite of financial protections designed to safeguard borrowers and their heirs. This chapter will explain what a non-recourse loan is, how mortgage insurance premiums (MIP) protect you, and the important consumer protections built into reverse mortgages to ensure a secure financial future.

1. What is a Non-Recourse Loan?

A reverse mortgage, specifically a HECM, is considered a non-recourse loan, which means that you or your heirs will never owe more than the value of your home at the time the loan is repaid. No matter how much interest accrues or how long you live in the home, the loan balance is capped by the home's appraised value when it is sold.

For example, if you take out a reverse mortgage and the loan balance grows to $300,000, but the home's value is only $250,000 at the time of sale, you or your heirs will only be responsible for repaying up to the appraised value of the home—$250,000. The remaining balance is covered by the FHA insurance, so you will not be personally liable for the difference.

Why It's Important:

This protection ensures that even if the real estate market declines or your loan balance grows over time, neither you nor your family will be financially burdened with paying off the loan beyond the value of your home. It offers peace of mind, especially for heirs, knowing they won't be stuck with an unaffordable loan debt after your passing.

2. Mortgage Insurance Premium (MIP)

To ensure that the non-recourse feature and other protections are upheld, reverse mortgage borrowers are required to pay Mortgage Insurance Premium (MIP). This insurance is provided by the Federal Housing Administration (FHA) and ensures that if the loan balance exceeds the value of your home when it's time to repay the loan, the FHA covers the difference, not you or your estate.

Two Types of MIP:

- Initial Mortgage Insurance Premium: This is a one-time fee paid upfront at closing. For most borrowers, the fee is 2% of the home's appraised value or the maximum lending limit, whichever is lower.

- Annual Mortgage Insurance Premium: In addition to the upfront premium, borrowers also pay an ongoing annual premium of 0.5% of the loan balance. This amount is added to the loan balance over time rather than paid out of pocket.

Why MIP Exists:

Mortgage insurance protects both the borrower and the lender. It ensures that the lender will be repaid, even if the loan balance exceeds the value of the home, while also protecting borrowers from owing more than the home's value. Without MIP, lenders would likely be more conservative in how much they allow borrowers to access, which would reduce the benefits of reverse mortgages for homeowners.

3. Consumer Protections

One of the most important aspects of reverse mortgages is the extensive consumer protections that have been built into the program. These protections are designed to ensure that homeowners understand the loan, are not exploited, and remain in good standing with their mortgage.

- Counseling Requirement:

    Before you can close on a reverse mortgage, you are required to participate in a counseling session with a HUD-approved counselor. This session is designed to ensure you fully understand the loan product, the associated costs, and your responsibilities. The counselor will also help you assess whether a reverse mortgage is truly the best option for your financial situation.

    This counseling session serves as a critical safeguard, helping to prevent seniors from taking out a reverse mortgage without fully understanding how it will impact their finances.

- No Foreclosure for Failure to Make Payments:

    Unlike traditional mortgages, reverse mortgages do not require monthly payments on the loan balance. As long as you continue to live in the home and meet your homeowner obligations—such as paying property taxes, homeowners insurance, and keeping the home in good condition—you cannot lose your home for failure to repay the loan.

    However, if you fail to meet these ongoing responsibilities (like paying property taxes or maintaining homeowners insurance), the lender has the right to foreclose on the home to recoup the loan balance. For this reason, it's critical that you stay current on these obligations.

- Protection for Non-Borrowing Spouses

    One of the key concerns for reverse mortgage borrowers is what happens if they have a younger spouse who does not qualify as a co-borrower. In cases where one spouse is younger than 62, they cannot be named on the loan as a borrower, but they may still be protected through the non-borrowing spouse provision.

    This protection allows the non-borrowing spouse to remain in the home after the borrowing spouse passes away or moves into long-term care, even though they were not listed on the reverse mortgage. They must continue to meet the homeownership obligations, such as paying taxes and insurance, but they will not be forced to sell the home or repay the loan during their lifetime.

- Caps on Fees and Interest

Reverse mortgages are highly regulated, which means there are caps on the interest rates and fees that lenders can charge. This helps protect borrowers from predatory lending practices and ensures the reverse mortgage remains a safe and viable option for older homeowners. Closing costs, interest rates, and servicing fees are all subject to FHA guidelines, so borrowers can rest assured that they won't face excessive charges.

4. Additional Safeguards

In addition to the key consumer protections outlined above, reverse mortgages come with a few more safeguards to ensure that you're making a well-informed financial decision:

- Right to Cancel: After closing on a reverse mortgage, borrowers have a three-day "right of rescission," which allows them to cancel the loan without penalty.

- Set-Asides for Key Obligations: If your financial assessment indicates you may have difficulty covering your property taxes and insurance, lenders can establish a Life Expectancy Set-Aside (LESA). This means a portion of your loan proceeds is set aside to cover these obligations, reducing the risk of defaulting on the loan.

- Regular Servicing: Reverse mortgage servicers are required to provide regular statements and maintain communication with borrowers. This includes annual updates on your loan balance, interest rates, and fees, ensuring you stay informed.

Conclusion

Reverse mortgages are designed with several key protections to ensure that homeowners can access their equity safely and securely. From the non-recourse loan feature to mortgage insurance premiums and various consumer protections, the program is built to shield borrowers from financial risk. Understanding these safeguards gives you confidence that a reverse mortgage can be a sound financial decision, not just for you, but for your heirs as well.

In the next chapter, we will explore the responsibilities you will need to maintain throughout the life of the loan and what to expect in terms of ongoing obligations.

CHAPTER 7

THE HOMEOWNER'S FINANCIAL RESPONSIBILITIES

While reverse mortgages offer the benefit of no monthly mortgage payments, homeowners still have important financial responsibilities to maintain throughout the life of the loan. In this chapter, we will cover what those obligations are, how your financial assessment determines eligibility, and what ongoing requirements you must meet to keep your reverse mortgage in good standing.

1. Ongoing Financial Obligations

Even though reverse mortgages do not require traditional loan payments, borrowers must still meet several key financial obligations to keep the loan from becoming due prematurely. Failure to comply with these responsibilities can result in default and potentially foreclosure. The main financial obligations are:

- Property Taxes: Homeowners are responsible for paying their property taxes on time. Falling behind on taxes is one of the most common reasons borrowers default on their reverse mortgage.

- Homeowners Insurance: You must maintain adequate homeowners insurance throughout the life of the loan. This protects both you and the lender by ensuring the home is covered in case of damage or other incidents.

- HOA Fees: If your home is part of a homeowner's association (HOA), you are required to pay HOA dues and comply with the association's rules.

- Home Maintenance and Repairs: The home must be kept in good condition. If the property falls into disrepair, the lender can require you to make repairs or declare the loan due. Regular maintenance, from roof repairs to general upkeep, is the borrower's responsibility.

2. Financial Assessment: What Lenders Review

Before approving a reverse mortgage, the lender will conduct a financial assessment. This assessment helps the lender determine whether you have the financial capacity to meet the ongoing responsibilities tied to your home, such as property taxes and insurance. This assessment is not the same as a traditional credit check, but it plays a critical role in determining whether you qualify for the loan.

The financial assessment includes:

- Credit History Review: Lenders will examine your credit history to see if you have a history of paying your bills on time. While a poor credit history won't necessarily disqualify you, it could trigger additional requirements like a Life Expectancy Set-Aside (LESA), where part of your loan proceeds is set aside to pay for taxes and insurance.

- Income and Cash Flow: Lenders will review your income and cash flow to ensure that you have enough resources to cover your ongoing obligations. This includes pensions, Social Security, and any other forms of income you receive. While reverse mortgages don't require income for repayment, lenders need to know you can still cover the costs of maintaining your home.

- Existing Debt and Liabilities: Your overall debt load will also be considered. If you have significant debts, it could affect your ability to meet your property-related obligations.

3. Life Expectancy Set-Aside (LESA)

If the lender determines through the financial assessment that you may have difficulty meeting your ongoing financial obligations (such as paying property taxes or insurance), they may require you to establish a Life Expectancy Set-Aside (LESA).

The LESA works by setting aside a portion of your loan proceeds to cover these costs. The funds are held by the lender and used to pay property taxes and homeowners insurance on your behalf, ensuring that you stay current on these critical payments and avoid defaulting on the loan.

Why LESA is Important:

The LESA is designed to protect both the borrower and the lender by ensuring that essential homeownership costs are always paid. It offers peace of mind for borrowers who might worry about managing their finances over time, knowing that these key expenses are handled.

4. Credit Requirements

While reverse mortgages do not rely heavily on credit scores the way traditional loans do, lenders still review your credit history to assess your ability to meet your financial obligations. If you have a poor credit history, it won't automatically disqualify you, but it can trigger additional requirements like setting aside loan proceeds for taxes and insurance.

Lenders are looking for signs that you are capable of managing ongoing expenses. If you have a history of late or missed payments on major bills (such as property taxes or insurance), the lender may impose restrictions or require a LESA.

5. Income Requirements

Unlike traditional mortgages, reverse mortgages do not require borrowers to have a high income because there are no monthly mortgage payments. However, lenders still want to ensure that you have enough income to meet the obligations of owning a home.

Common sources of income reviewed by lenders include:
- Social Security benefits
- Pension payments
- Investment income
- Rental income (if applicable)

The purpose of reviewing income is to ensure that you will be able to afford necessary expenses like property taxes, insurance, and home maintenance. If your income is insufficient, the lender may require a LESA to cover these obligations.

6. Home Maintenance and Repairs

One of the most critical ongoing obligations is maintaining the condition of the home. Lenders require that the home remain in good condition because it serves as collateral for the loan. Regular upkeep and repairs, from roof maintenance to basic repairs, are the homeowner's responsibility.

Failure to maintain the home could result in the lender requiring you to make repairs or, in extreme cases, declaring the loan due. If major repairs are necessary at the time you take out the reverse mortgage, the lender may set aside funds from your loan proceeds to cover the cost of those repairs.

7. What Happens if You Fail to Meet Obligations?

If you fall behind on your property taxes, insurance payments, or other financial obligations, the lender may take steps to rectify the situation. The lender may:

- Use funds from the LESA (if established) to cover missed payments.

- Work with you to set up a repayment plan for missed taxes or insurance.

- Declare the loan due and payable, which could result in foreclosure if the issue is not resolved.

It's essential to stay current on all property-related obligations to avoid the risk of defaulting on your reverse mortgage.

Conclusion

While reverse mortgages eliminate the need for monthly mortgage payments, they come with important financial responsibilities that homeowners must meet. From paying property taxes and insurance to keeping the home in good condition, these obligations are key to maintaining the loan. The lender's financial assessment, including a review of your income and credit history, ensures that you are equipped to meet these ongoing responsibilities. For borrowers who may struggle to manage these costs, the LESA provides an additional layer of protection by setting aside funds to cover property-related expenses.

In the next chapter, we will explore special loan features such as the line of credit and how it grows over time.

CHAPTER 8

SPECIAL LOAN FEATURES: LINE OF CREDIT AND GROWTH

One of the unique aspects of a reverse mortgage is the option to receive your loan proceeds as a line of credit, which offers more flexibility compared to a lump sum or monthly payments. In addition, the reverse mortgage line of credit has a distinct and powerful feature—it grows over time. This chapter will explain how the reverse mortgage line of credit works, why it's different from traditional lines of credit, and how the growth feature can benefit you over the long term.

1. What Is the Reverse Mortgage Line of Credit?

The line of credit option allows reverse mortgage borrowers to access their home's equity when they need it, without taking all the funds upfront. Unlike a lump-sum payout, which gives you a set amount of money all at once, or monthly payments, which provide a fixed amount each month, the line of credit allows you to withdraw money as needed.

The amount of the line of credit is determined at the start of the reverse mortgage and is based on factors such as your age, home value, and current interest rates. You can withdraw from this line of credit whenever you need funds, and you only accrue interest on the amount you've borrowed, not the full line of credit.

Why This Is Valuable:

The reverse mortgage line of credit offers flexibility and control. You don't need to draw all your available funds immediately, which means that the unused portion of your line of credit is available for future expenses—whether for unexpected emergencies, home repairs, or supplementing your retirement income.

2. How the Line of Credit Grows Over Time

One of the most significant and unique features of the reverse mortgage line of credit is that it grows over time. This is unlike a traditional home equity line of credit (HELOC), where the available credit remains the same unless you borrow more or pay it down. In a reverse mortgage, as long as you leave funds unused, the available balance in your line of credit will increase over time.

Why Does It Grow?

The growth of the line of credit is directly tied to the interest rate on your loan. As time passes, the unused portion of your line of credit increases at the same rate as the interest charged on the loan. This means that your available credit expands over time, giving you more money to access in the future, even if your home's value stays the same or decreases.

For example, if you have $100,000 in your reverse mortgage line of credit and you don't touch it for several years, that amount will grow, potentially providing much more than the initial $100,000. This growth can be particularly helpful for homeowners who want a financial safety net later in life or anticipate large future expenses.

3. Comparing the Reverse Mortgage Line of Credit to a Traditional HELOC

It's helpful to understand how the reverse mortgage line of credit differs from a traditional home equity line of credit (HELOC). Both products allow you to borrow against the equity in your home, but there are key differences in how they work:

Reverse Mortgage Line of Credit:

- No Monthly Repayment Requirement: Unlike a HELOC, you are not required to make monthly payments. Interest accrues over time, and repayment is deferred until the loan becomes due (usually when you sell the home, move, or pass away).

- Credit Line Growth: As mentioned, the unused portion of your reverse mortgage line of credit grows over time, giving you access to more funds in the future.

- No Risk of Frozen Credit: With a traditional HELOC, the lender can freeze your credit line or reduce your available credit if your home's value declines or the market changes. This isn't the case with a reverse mortgage line of credit—your access to funds remains secure as long as you meet the terms of the loan (paying taxes, insurance, and maintaining the home).

Traditional HELOC:

- Monthly Repayments Required: A HELOC requires you to make monthly payments of both principal and interest, which could become a burden if your financial situation changes.

- No Growth: The available credit in a HELOC remains fixed unless you repay part of what you've borrowed, and there's no built-in growth feature.

- Risk of Credit Line Freeze: If property values drop or your credit score changes, the lender can freeze your HELOC, reducing or eliminating your access to funds.

4. Strategic Uses of the Line of Credit

Because the line of credit grows over time, many financial advisors suggest using it as a financial planning tool rather than drawing from it immediately. Here are a few ways you can strategically use the reverse mortgage line of credit:

- Emergency Fund: The line of credit can serve as a safety net for unexpected expenses, such as medical bills, home repairs, or other unforeseen financial needs. Since the available funds grow over time, the longer you leave the line of credit untouched, the more money you'll have available if a financial emergency arises.

- Supplement Retirement Income: If your retirement savings or other income sources fall short, you can use the line of credit to supplement your income without having to sell your home or draw from other investments.

- Delaying Social Security Benefits: Some retirees use the reverse mortgage line of credit to cover living expenses while delaying Social Security benefits. Delaying Social Security can lead to larger monthly payments in the future, and the growing line of credit ensures you have a backup source of funds in the meantime.

- Tax-Deferred Strategy: Since reverse mortgage proceeds are not considered taxable income, using the line of credit can help you manage your taxable income. This can be especially useful for retirees who want to avoid drawing on tax-deferred retirement accounts early, which can increase their taxable income.

5. No Obligation to Use the Line of Credit

Another advantage of the reverse mortgage line of credit is that you're under no obligation to use the funds. If your financial situation improves or if you don't need to access the credit, it will simply continue to grow. There are no penalties for leaving the line of credit untouched, making it a flexible financial tool that adapts to your changing needs over time.

6. What Happens When the Loan Becomes Due?

The reverse mortgage line of credit remains available as long as you live in the home, maintain it, and meet your financial obligations (like paying property taxes and homeowners insurance). When a maturity event occurs—such as selling the home, moving out permanently, or passing away—the loan becomes due. At that time, the funds you've drawn, along with any accrued interest, must be repaid.

If the loan balance exceeds the value of the home, the non-recourse feature of the reverse mortgage ensures that you or your heirs will never owe more than the home is worth.

Conclusion

The reverse mortgage line of credit offers a unique financial tool that grows over time, providing flexibility and a powerful hedge against future financial needs. Whether used as an emergency fund, a supplement to retirement income, or a strategy for delaying other income sources, the growing line of credit provides significant advantages that traditional HELOCs and lump-sum payouts cannot match.

In the next chapter, we will explore how interest rates affect reverse mortgages, covering the differences between fixed and adjustable rates and how they influence your loan options.

CHAPTER 9

UNDERSTANDING LOAN OPTIONS: FIXED VS. ADJUSTABLE RATES

When you take out a reverse mortgage, you'll need to choose between two types of interest rates: fixed rates or adjustable rates. Each option comes with its own advantages and trade-offs, and understanding how they work is key to making the right decision for your financial needs. In this chapter, we will explore both fixed and adjustable-rate reverse mortgages, the purpose of the expected rate, and how these choices can impact your loan over time.

1. Fixed-Rate Reverse Mortgages

A fixed-rate reverse mortgage locks in a consistent interest rate for the life of the loan. This means that from the moment you take out the reverse mortgage, the interest rate will remain the same, regardless of changes in the market.

Advantages of Fixed-Rate Reverse Mortgages:

- Predictability: A fixed-rate reverse mortgage gives you certainty. You'll know exactly how much interest will accrue over the life of the loan, which makes financial planning easier.

- No Surprises: With a fixed rate, you don't have to worry about fluctuations in interest rates that could increase the cost of your loan over time.

Limitations of Fixed-Rate Reverse Mortgages:

- Lump Sum Payout: One significant limitation of fixed-rate reverse mortgages is that you must take all your loan proceeds as a lump sum. This means you'll receive all the available funds upfront and won't have the flexibility to draw money over time, as you would with a line of credit.

- Potential Over-Borrowing: Because you receive all the loan proceeds at once, there's a risk of over-borrowing. Some borrowers may be tempted to take more than they need, which can deplete equity faster and reduce the amount of home equity available for future needs.

2. Adjustable-Rate Reverse Mortgages

An adjustable-rate reverse mortgage (ARM) allows your interest rate to change over time, depending on the current market conditions. With this option, your interest rate may rise or fall over the life of the loan, and the amount of interest that accrues can fluctuate accordingly.

Advantages of Adjustable-Rate Reverse Mortgages:
- Flexible Payout Options: Unlike fixed-rate loans, adjustable-rate reverse mortgages allow for multiple payout options. You can choose to take a lump sum, monthly payments, or set up a line of credit, which offers flexibility to access funds as needed. This is particularly beneficial for those who want to draw on their loan proceeds over time.

- Growing Line of Credit: If you choose the line of credit option with an adjustable rate, your available credit can grow over time (as discussed in Chapter 8), giving you access to more funds in the future.

Limitations of Adjustable-Rate Reverse Mortgages:

- Uncertainty: The main drawback of an adjustable rate is that you won't know exactly how much interest will accrue over the life of the loan. If interest rates rise, the loan balance can grow faster than expected, potentially using up more of your home equity.

- Fluctuating Costs: As rates change, so do your costs. While the reverse mortgage doesn't require monthly payments, rising interest rates will increase the total amount owed when the loan becomes due.

3. Choosing Between Fixed and Adjustable Rates

When deciding between a fixed or adjustable rate for your reverse mortgage, it's important to consider your financial goals and how you plan to use the loan proceeds.
When Fixed Rates Make Sense:

- You want the security of a predictable interest rate and know you'll be using the funds for a large one-time expense, such as paying off an existing mortgage or medical bills.

- You're comfortable with receiving a lump sum and don't need future access to additional loan proceeds.

When Adjustable Rates Make Sense:
- You want the flexibility of different payout options, such as receiving monthly payments or setting up a line of credit.

- You're interested in accessing your home equity over time and want to benefit from the growing line of credit feature, which is only available with adjustable-rate reverse mortgages.

- You're comfortable with some degree of uncertainty and are prepared for interest rate fluctuations over the life of the loan.

4. Understanding the Expected Interest Rate

In addition to the interest rate you lock in, reverse mortgages also involve an important concept known as the expected interest rate. This is an estimate of what the interest rate will average over the life of the loan. While the expected rate doesn't affect how much interest you'll actually pay, it plays a critical role in determining how much money you can borrow upfront.

How the Expected Rate Works:

- The expected interest rate is used to calculate your principal limit, which is the maximum amount you're allowed to borrow. The lower the expected rate, the more money you can borrow, and vice versa.

- If the expected rate is high, the assumption is that more interest will accrue over the life of the loan, reducing the amount of equity you can initially access. Conversely, a lower expected rate allows you to borrow more because the loan balance is expected to grow more slowly.

Why the Expected Rate Is Important:

Even though the expected rate doesn't directly impact your interest charges (since actual interest rates may fluctuate with an adjustable-rate loan), it plays a vital role in determining how much you can access when you first take out the reverse mortgage. Understanding how the expected rate influences your borrowing capacity is key to making an informed decision about your loan.

5. How Interest Rates Affect Loan Proceeds

Both the interest rate you lock in (fixed or adjustable) and the expected rate impact the total amount of equity you can access through your reverse mortgage. Here's how:

- Fixed-Rate Loans: Because the rate is locked in and the lender is assuming they'll be charging the same interest for the life of the loan, the amount you can borrow may be slightly lower than with an adjustable-rate loan.

- Adjustable-Rate Loans: These typically offer a bit more flexibility in how much you can borrow initially, especially if the expected interest rate is low. The trade-off, however, is the uncertainty around how rates will fluctuate in the future, potentially increasing the loan balance over time.

Conclusion

Choosing between a fixed-rate and adjustable-rate reverse mortgage depends on your financial needs, risk tolerance, and how you plan to use the loan proceeds. Fixed-rate loans offer security and predictability, but come with less flexibility. Adjustable-rate loans provide the freedom of flexible payout options and the potential for a growing line of credit, but carry the risk of fluctuating interest rates. Additionally, understanding the expected rate is crucial for calculating how much money you'll be able to borrow upfront.

In the next chapter, we will explore how to lock in your interest rate and what options you have for receiving your reverse mortgage proceeds.

CHAPTER 10
PAYOUT STRUCTURES AND LOCKING IN YOUR INTEREST RATE

Once you've decided on whether to go with a fixed or adjustable-rate reverse mortgage, the next step is to understand your payout options and how to lock in your interest rate. The payout structure you choose will influence how and when you receive your loan proceeds, while locking in your interest rate will determine how much interest accrues over the life of your loan. In this chapter, we will explore the different payout structures available and how to secure your interest rate based on your financial needs.

1. Payout Structures: How to Receive Your Funds

One of the key benefits of reverse mortgages is the flexibility they offer in terms of how you receive your loan proceeds. Depending on whether you choose a fixed or adjustable-rate reverse mortgage, there are several payout structures to choose from. These options allow you to tailor the loan to meet your specific financial goals, whether you need immediate access to cash or want to set up a line of credit for future needs.

1. Lump-Sum Payment

With a lump-sum payment, you receive all of your reverse mortgage proceeds at once, immediately after closing. This payout option is typically only available with fixed-rate reverse mortgages and is ideal for borrowers who need a large sum of money for a significant one-time expense, such as paying off an existing mortgage, covering medical bills, or funding home renovations.

Advantages of a Lump Sum:

- You receive all the available loan proceeds upfront.
- Predictable interest rates and repayment structure with a fixed rate.

Disadvantages of a Lump Sum:

- Once you take out the funds, you won't have access to additional money in the future.
- All interest accrues on the full loan balance from the start, reducing home equity faster.

2. Line of Credit

The line of credit option is one of the most flexible payout structures available, but it's only offered with adjustable-rate reverse mortgages. With a line of credit, you can access funds as needed, and any unused portion of the credit line grows over time (as covered in Chapter 8).

Advantages of a Line of Credit:

- You only accrue interest on the amount you've withdrawn, not the full loan balance.
- Unused funds grow over time, providing more money for future expenses.
- It offers flexibility to meet changing financial needs.

Disadvantages of a Line of Credit:

- The adjustable interest rate means that the interest rate on the borrowed funds can increase over time.
- It may require more careful financial planning to avoid over-borrowing.

3. Monthly Payments (Tenure or Term)

Monthly payments allow you to receive your loan proceeds in fixed installments over a set period. There are two primary types of monthly payments:

- Tenure Payments: You receive monthly payments for as long as you live in the home as your primary residence. This is a good option for borrowers who want a consistent stream of income throughout their retirement.

- Term Payments: You receive monthly payments for a set number of years, such as 10 or 15 years. This is ideal for those who anticipate needing financial assistance for a specific period, like during early retirement.

Advantages of Monthly Payments:

- Provides a reliable source of income over time.

- You can choose a term that suits your financial needs (lifelong or for a set period).

Disadvantages of Monthly Payments:

- If you opt for term payments and outlive the set period, you won't have access to additional funds once the term ends.

4. Combination of Payout Options

If you want more flexibility, some reverse mortgages allow you to combine payout options. For example, you might choose to take a portion of the loan proceeds as a lump sum upfront and set up the rest as a line of credit or monthly payments. This strategy can provide the immediate cash you need while preserving funds for future use.

Advantages of a Combination Option:

- Flexibility to meet both immediate and long-term financial goals.

- Customizable to suit your unique needs, whether for large expenses, emergency funds, or retirement income.

Disadvantages of a Combination Option:

- Managing multiple payout streams can require careful financial planning.

- Interest accrues on the lump sum portion right away, reducing future equity.

2. Locking in Your Interest Rate

Once you've decided on your payout structure, you'll need to lock in your interest rate. The timing of when you lock in the rate can significantly impact the total cost of your loan and how much interest accrues over time. Here's how to go about it:

Fixed-Rate Reverse Mortgages

For fixed-rate reverse mortgages, your interest rate is locked in when the loan closes. This means that the rate you agree to at the time of closing will remain the same throughout the life of the loan, regardless of changes in market conditions.

How to Lock Your Fixed Rate:

Fixed-rate reverse mortgages are straightforward in terms of interest rate locking. Once you've chosen the fixed-rate option and closed on the loan, your interest rate is locked in automatically. There is no risk of future rate fluctuations, which makes financial planning simpler.

Adjustable-Rate Reverse Mortgages

For adjustable-rate reverse mortgages, your interest rate will fluctuate over time, but the initial rate at closing will be locked in for the first adjustment period. After that, the interest rate can change periodically based on market conditions.

How to Lock Your Adjustable Rate:

- Adjustable-rate reverse mortgages are tied to specific financial indexes, such as the LIBOR (London Interbank Offered Rate) or CMT (Constant Maturity Treasury), which means the rate can change depending on market movements.

- You won't lock in a permanent rate with adjustable loans, but the initial rate at closing will be set for a short period, often a year or more, before it adjusts.

Choosing the Right Time to Lock:

The timing of when you lock in your adjustable rate can impact how favorable the initial rate will be. It's worth consulting with your reverse mortgage lender or financial advisor to determine when market conditions might provide the most advantageous rates.

3. Factors to Consider When Locking Your Rate

The choice of when to lock your rate—whether fixed or adjustable—can be influenced by several factors:

- Current Interest Rates: If interest rates are low, it may be a good time to lock in your rate. For fixed-rate mortgages, this locks in a favorable rate for the entire loan period. For adjustable-rate mortgages, a lower initial rate gives you more room before potential rate increases.

- Market Outlook: If interest rates are expected to rise in the future, it may make sense to lock in your rate sooner rather than later. However, if rates are predicted to drop, you might choose to wait with an adjustable-rate loan.

- Your Financial Goals: Your choice of when to lock your rate should align with your financial needs and goals. If you prefer long-term stability, locking in a fixed rate may be the best option. If you're looking for flexibility and potentially lower initial rates, an adjustable rate might be better suited for your situation.

Conclusion

Choosing how to receive your reverse mortgage proceeds and locking in your interest rate are critical decisions that will shape your financial strategy moving forward. Whether you prefer the simplicity of a lump sum, the flexibility of a line of credit, or the steady income from monthly payments, there's a payout structure that fits your needs. Similarly, deciding when and how to lock your interest rate—whether fixed or adjustable—can help ensure your loan aligns with your long-term goals.

In the next chapter, we will take a closer look at the costs associated with reverse mortgages and what you can expect in terms of fees and expenses.

CHAPTER 11

WHAT HAPPENS TO THE HOME AFTER DEATH

One of the most common questions homeowners and their families ask when considering a reverse mortgage is: What happens to the home after I pass away? A reverse mortgage allows you to access the equity in your home while you're alive, but like all loans, it must eventually be repaid. In this chapter, we'll discuss what happens to the home when the borrower passes away, the options available to heirs, and how the repayment process works.

1. The Loan Becomes Due

A reverse mortgage does not need to be repaid as long as you live in the home as your primary residence, keep up with property taxes, insurance, and home maintenance. However, once you pass away, the loan reaches what is known as a maturity event, which triggers the repayment process. The reverse mortgage becomes due, and your heirs or estate must take action to settle the loan balance.

Typically, the reverse mortgage loan is paid off through the sale of the home, though there are other options available, which we'll explore in this chapter.

2. Options for Heirs

When a reverse mortgage borrower passes away, the heirs or estate have several options for handling the home and the outstanding loan balance. It's essential that your heirs understand these choices and know what to expect when the time comes.

Here are the key options:

Sell the Home

The most common way to repay a reverse mortgage is by selling the home. Heirs can sell the home, and the proceeds from the sale are used to pay off the loan balance. If the home is worth more than the loan balance, the remaining equity goes to the heirs.

- Non-Recourse Feature: If the loan balance is higher than the home's value (for example, if the real estate market has declined), the non-recourse feature of reverse mortgages protects your heirs. They will not be responsible for any difference between the sale price of the home and the loan balance. The FHA insurance will cover any shortfall, ensuring that heirs are not left with debt.

Keep the Home

If your heirs want to keep the home, they have the option to pay off the reverse mortgage balance using other funds. This could involve paying the loan balance in cash, refinancing the home with a traditional mortgage, or using other resources to settle the debt.

- Loan Balance vs. Home Value: If the loan balance is less than the value of the home, your heirs will need to repay the full loan balance to retain ownership. If the loan balance exceeds the home's value, they can pay off the loan at 95% of the home's appraised value, even if that amount is lower than the outstanding loan balance. This provision ensures that heirs aren't forced to pay more than the home is worth.

Walk Away from the Home

If your heirs do not want to sell the home or keep it, they have the option to simply walk away. In this case, the lender will take possession of the home through foreclosure. Since reverse mortgages are non-recourse loans, your heirs will not owe any additional money beyond the home's value, and they are not responsible for the debt. The home becomes the lender's property, and the loan is considered settled.

3. The Repayment Process

After the borrower passes away, the lender will notify the heirs or the estate that the reverse mortgage is due. The heirs typically have a period of time to decide how to proceed, usually around 6-12 months, although this can vary depending on the lender and circumstances.

Step-by-Step Repayment Process:

1. Notification: The lender will notify the heirs or estate that the loan has matured and is now due.

2. Decision Time: The heirs have several months to decide whether to sell the home, keep it by repaying the loan, or let the lender take possession of the home.

3. Appraisal (if needed): If the heirs want to keep the home or pay off the loan, the home's current market value may be appraised to determine whether the loan balance exceeds the home's worth.

4. Repayment: If the heirs choose to sell the home, they will arrange for the sale, and the loan will be paid off from the proceeds. If they choose to keep the home, they will need to pay off the loan directly or through refinancing.

4. Non-Recourse Protection for Heirs

As mentioned earlier, reverse mortgages are non-recourse loans, meaning that neither the borrower nor their heirs can owe more than the value of the home. This protection is critical because it ensures that heirs will not be stuck with an unpaid debt if the loan balance is greater than the home's market value.

For example, if the loan balance is $300,000 but the home's value is only $250,000, your heirs can sell the home for $250,000, and the FHA insurance will cover the difference. Heirs are not responsible for paying off the remaining $50,000.

5. What Happens to the Home if There Are Multiple Heirs?

If you have multiple heirs, the process for dealing with the home after death can be a bit more complex. Typically, the estate's executor (or trustee, if a living trust is involved) will be responsible for coordinating the sale or repayment of the reverse mortgage. All heirs will need to agree on how to proceed—whether to sell the home, keep it, or let the lender take possession.

In some cases, one heir may want to keep the home while others prefer to sell. In these situations, the heir who wants to keep the home can pay off the reverse mortgage using other funds or refinancing, allowing them to retain ownership.

6. Communicating with Your Heirs

Because reverse mortgages involve your home and can have a significant financial impact, it's important to discuss your plans with your heirs before the loan becomes due. Make sure they understand the options available to them and how they can handle the home when you pass away. Clear communication can help prevent confusion and ensure a smoother process for your family.

Conclusion

When a reverse mortgage borrower passes away, the loan becomes due, and heirs must decide what to do with the home. Fortunately, reverse mortgages offer flexibility, allowing heirs to sell the home, keep it by paying off the loan, or walk away without any financial liability beyond the home's value. The non-recourse feature protects heirs from owing more than the home is worth, offering peace of mind to both borrowers and their families.

In the next chapter, we will discuss the homeowner's obligations while living with a reverse mortgage and what they need to do to maintain their loan in good standing.

CHAPTER 12

Reverse Mortgage Costs Explained

Reverse mortgages come with various costs, many of which are added to the loan balance rather than paid out of pocket. It's essential to understand the different types of expenses associated with reverse mortgages, how they affect your available equity, and which costs you will need to cover immediately. In this chapter, we'll break down the key costs that are added to your loan balance, the few out-of-pocket expenses you need to plan for, and the ongoing responsibilities that come with maintaining your reverse mortgage.

1. Costs Added to the Loan Balance

Most reverse mortgage fees are added directly to your loan balance. This means you don't have to pay them upfront; however, they will reduce the amount of home equity available to you and accrue interest over time. These include:

- Origination Fees: The origination fee is charged by the lender for processing the reverse mortgage and managing the administrative aspects of setting up the loan. The fee varies depending on the lender and the value of your home.

- HECM Origination Fees: For Home Equity Conversion Mortgages (HECM), the maximum origination fee is capped by the Federal Housing Administration (FHA):
  - 2% of the first $200,000 of your home's appraised value.
  - 1% of the amount above $200,000.
  - The total origination fee is capped at $6,000.

2. Mortgage Insurance Premium (MIP)

A significant part of the reverse mortgage cost is the Mortgage Insurance Premium (MIP), which is required for HECM loans. This insurance protects both you and the lender, ensuring that if your loan balance exceeds the value of your home, neither you nor your heirs will be responsible for the difference.

- Initial MIP: This is a one-time charge of 2% of your home's appraised value or the FHA lending limit (whichever is lower). This cost is added to the loan balance at closing.

- Annual MIP: In addition to the initial MIP, an annual premium of 0.5% of the outstanding loan balance is added to the loan each year. This ensures continuous protection for you and the lender over the life of the loan.

3. Closing Costs

Just like with any mortgage, reverse mortgages come with closing costs, which cover various fees related to finalizing the loan. These costs are typically added to your loan balance and include:

- Title Insurance: Protects both you and the lender in case there are disputes over ownership or liens against the property.

- Title Search: A thorough review to ensure the property's title is clear and free from legal encumbrances.

- Tax Stamps and Recording Fees: These are government-imposed fees for registering the new loan with your local authorities.

- Other Fees: Lenders may also charge for notary services, document preparation, and credit checks, all of which are necessary to complete the transaction.

Why These Costs Matter:

By being rolled into the loan balance, these fees will accumulate interest over time, reducing the remaining equity in your home. It's essential to account for these costs when determining how much equity you'll have access to through your reverse mortgage.

4. Out-of-Pocket Costs

While most fees are added to your loan balance, there are a few costs you will need to pay out of pocket before your reverse mortgage can be finalized. These include:

- Appraisal Fee: An appraisal of your home is required to determine its current market value. This fee typically ranges from $300 to $600 and must be paid upfront. The appraisal ensures the lender knows how much equity is available for the reverse mortgage and identifies any necessary repairs before the loan is approved.

- HUD-Approved Counseling: Before obtaining a reverse mortgage, you are required to undergo HUD-approved counseling to ensure you fully understand the loan and its implications. This counseling session typically costs around $125 and is paid directly to the counseling agency. It's an essential step to ensure borrowers are well-informed and protected.

- Ongoing Costs Added to the Loan Balance

In addition to the initial fees, several costs will continue to be added to your loan balance over the life of the loan. These include:

- Annual Mortgage Insurance Premium (MIP): As mentioned earlier, the annual MIP is added to the loan each year at a rate of 0.5% of the outstanding loan balance. This fee is critical in maintaining the protection provided by FHA insurance, ensuring that neither you nor your heirs will owe more than the home's value when the loan becomes due.

- Interest: Interest on a reverse mortgage accrues over time and is added to the loan balance. The amount of interest you pay will depend on whether you chose a fixed-rate or adjustable-rate reverse mortgage.

- Fixed-Rate Loans: Your interest rate remains the same for the life of the loan, providing predictability.

- Adjustable-Rate Loans: The interest rate may change over time based on market conditions, which could result in either higher or lower interest accrual.

Interest accrues on the amount of loan proceeds you've drawn, meaning if you take a lump sum or draw on a line of credit, the interest will accumulate based on the amount you've borrowed.

- Servicing Fees: Lenders may charge servicing fees to manage your loan over time. These fees typically cover the cost of administrative tasks such as sending out loan statements, managing disbursements, and responding to borrower inquiries.

  - Servicing fees are often bundled into the loan balance and typically range from $25 to $35 per month.

- Homeowner Responsibilities: While reverse mortgages provide the benefit of no monthly loan payments, you are still responsible for several ongoing home-related expenses. These costs are not added to your loan balance and must be paid directly by you to keep the loan in good standing:

  - Property Taxes: You must continue to pay your property taxes. If you fall behind on property taxes, it could result in the lender calling the loan due, potentially leading to foreclosure. Staying current on taxes is a critical responsibility.

    - Homeowners Insurance: Maintaining homeowners insurance is also mandatory. This ensures that both you and the lender are protected in case of damage to the property. If you fail to keep the insurance active, it could result in loan default.

    - Home Maintenance: You are required to keep the home in good repair. This ensures the property retains its value, as the home serves as collateral for the loan. If the home falls into disrepair, the lender may require you to make repairs to avoid default.

o   HOA Fees (If Applicable): If your home is part of a homeowners association (HOA), you must continue to pay HOA dues. These fees ensure you comply with association rules and maintain community standards.

o   The Total Cost Picture: The total cost of your reverse mortgage depends on several factors: the amount of time you hold the loan, the interest rate, and the fees involved. Since many costs are added to the loan balance, they will accrue interest over time, reducing the remaining equity in your home.

Key Points to Consider:

- Costs added to the loan balance include origination fees, MIP, interest, and servicing fees.

- Out-of-pocket costs include the appraisal fee and HUD-approved counseling.

- Homeowner obligations include property taxes, insurance, and maintenance, which must be paid directly.

Conclusion

Understanding the costs associated with a reverse mortgage is essential for making an informed decision. While most of the fees are added to your loan balance, reducing your available equity, some out-of-pocket expenses must be paid upfront. Additionally, maintaining your home and staying current on taxes and insurance is vital to keeping the loan in good standing. By planning for these costs, you can ensure a smoother reverse mortgage experience.

In the next chapter, we'll explore the borrower protections in place, such as counseling requirements and the non-recourse feature that ensures you'll never owe more than your home's value.

CHAPTER 13

Protecting the Borrower:
Counseling and Non-Borrowing Spouse

Reverse mortgages come with a number of built-in protections to ensure that borrowers fully understand their financial commitments and are safeguarded in various situations. One of the key protections is mandatory HUD-approved counseling, which helps borrowers make informed decisions. Additionally, special provisions exist for non-borrowing spouses under the age of 62, allowing them to remain in the home after the borrowing spouse passes away. In this chapter, we'll explore these critical protections and how they benefit borrowers and their families.

1. HUD-Approved Counseling: Why It's Required

A reverse mortgage is a major financial commitment, and the government mandates that all borrowers participate in HUD-approved counseling before taking out the loan. This is designed to ensure that borrowers fully understand the reverse mortgage, how it works, and its long-term implications.

The Purpose of Counseling

The primary goal of counseling is to provide borrowers with the knowledge they need to make an informed decision. Since reverse mortgages can be complex, especially for older homeowners, this counseling session is an opportunity to:

- Ensure you understand how reverse mortgages work, including the costs, benefits, and risks.

- Review the different payout options (lump sum, line of credit, monthly payments) and help you decide which best fits your financial situation.

- Discuss alternatives to a reverse mortgage, such as downsizing or a traditional home equity loan.

- Ensure you are aware of the ongoing financial obligations, such as property taxes, homeowners insurance, and home maintenance, and understand the consequences of failing to meet these obligations.

How Counseling Works

- Cost: Counseling typically costs around $125, though some organizations may offer the service at a reduced rate or even for free.

- Process: You can complete the session in person, over the phone, or online. The counselor will review your financial situation, discuss your goals, and walk you through the reverse mortgage process.

- Outcome: At the end of the session, the counselor will provide you with a certificate confirming that you have completed counseling. This certificate is required before you can proceed with the reverse mortgage application.

Why Counseling is Important

Counseling protects borrowers from making uninformed or hasty decisions. By ensuring that you fully understand the loan, its costs, and your responsibilities, the process helps reduce the risk of misunderstandings or regret later on. It also ensures that you are aware of alternative options that may better fit your needs if a reverse mortgage isn't the right choice for you.

2. Non-Borrowing Spouse Protections

One of the most significant concerns for couples considering a reverse mortgage is what happens to the non-borrowing spouse if the borrowing spouse passes away. This is especially important in cases where one spouse is under 62 years old and, therefore, ineligible to be listed as a borrower on the reverse mortgage.

Fortunately, the HECM program includes protections for non-borrowing spouses, ensuring that they can remain in the home after the borrowing spouse dies or moves into long-term care.

Who is Considered a Non-Borrowing Spouse?

A non-borrowing spouse is a spouse who is not included on the reverse mortgage loan because they are younger than 62. In some cases, a non-borrowing spouse may be over 62 but chooses not to be listed as a borrower for other reasons.

Non-borrowing spouses do not have access to the reverse mortgage funds, but the HECM program includes protections that allow them to stay in the home after the borrower's death or departure.

Protections for Non-Borrowing Spouses

The 2014 changes to the HECM program introduced safeguards to ensure that non-borrowing spouses can continue to live in the home even after the borrowing spouse passes away or moves into long-term care. These protections include:

- Deferral of Loan Repayment: When the borrowing spouse passes away, the reverse mortgage loan does not immediately become due. Instead, the loan repayment is deferred as long as the non-borrowing spouse continues to live in the home as their primary residence, maintains the property, and stays current on taxes and insurance.

- Right to Remain in the Home: As long as the non-borrowing spouse complies with the terms of the reverse mortgage (such as keeping up with property taxes, homeowners insurance, and home maintenance), they can remain in the home indefinitely, without the risk of foreclosure.

Requirements to Qualify for Non-Borrowing Spouse Protections

To ensure that the non-borrowing spouse is protected, certain conditions must be met:

- The spouse must have been married to the borrowing spouse at the time the reverse mortgage was taken out.

- The non-borrowing spouse must be living in the home as their primary residence at the time of the borrowing spouse's death or departure.

- The non-borrowing spouse must comply with all the same responsibilities as the borrower, such as paying property taxes and insurance, and maintaining the home.

These protections ensure that non-borrowing spouses are not forced to move out of the home after the borrowing spouse dies, providing peace of mind for couples considering a reverse mortgage.

Limitations of Non-Borrowing Spouse Protections

While these protections are valuable, there are some limitations that non-borrowing spouses should be aware of:

- No Access to Loan Proceeds: Non-borrowing spouses are not entitled to receive any of the loan proceeds after the borrowing spouse's death. This means that they cannot draw on any remaining funds from the reverse mortgage.

- Loan Balance Continues to Grow: Even though the loan repayment is deferred, interest and mortgage insurance premiums will continue to accrue on the loan balance. This can reduce the amount of equity available when the loan is eventually repaid.

3. Eligible vs. Ineligible Non-Borrowing Spouse

In certain cases, a spouse may be considered an ineligible non-borrowing spouse, meaning they do not qualify for the protections discussed above. This usually occurs when the spouse was not married to the borrower at the time the reverse mortgage was taken out, or if they were not living in the home as their primary residence.

- Eligible Non-Borrowing Spouse: A spouse who was married to the borrower at the time the reverse mortgage was originated and who meets all the eligibility criteria for protection under the HECM program.

- Ineligible Non-Borrowing Spouse: A spouse who either married the borrower after the reverse mortgage was taken out or does not meet the residency requirements. In this case, the ineligible spouse is not entitled to remain in the home after the borrower's death or departure, and the loan would become due.

4. Communicating with Your Spouse and Family

Because reverse mortgages can affect what happens to your home after death, it's important to have open conversations with your spouse and family members before proceeding with the loan. Ensure that everyone understands the rights and responsibilities of both the borrowing and non-borrowing spouse, and how the loan will impact the family's financial situation in the long term.

Conclusion

Borrower protections are one of the most important aspects of reverse mortgages. Mandatory HUD-approved counseling ensures that borrowers fully understand their financial responsibilities and options, while non-borrowing spouse protections provide security for couples, ensuring that a surviving spouse can remain in the home even after the borrowing spouse passes away. By understanding these protections and how they apply, you can make an informed decision about whether a reverse mortgage is the right choice for you and your family.

In the next chapter, we'll explore refinancing options for reverse mortgages and how homeowners can manage their reverse mortgage over time.

CHAPTER 14

HECM and Refinancing Options

A reverse mortgage can be a long-term financial tool, but over time, homeowners may want to revisit their loan to adjust to changing financial circumstances. Whether you're looking to refinance your reverse mortgage for better terms or use a reverse mortgage to purchase a new home, understanding your Home Equity Conversion Mortgage (HECM) refinancing options is key. In this chapter, we'll explore HECM-to-HECM refinancing, HECM for purchase, and how these options can fit into your broader financial planning strategy.

1. HECM-to-HECM Refinancing

Just like a traditional mortgage, a reverse mortgage can be refinanced if your situation changes or if better loan terms become available. A HECM-to-HECM refinance allows homeowners to take out a new HECM reverse mortgage to replace an existing one, often with the goal of accessing more equity or taking advantage of more favorable terms.

When Does Refinancing Make Sense?

Refinancing a HECM reverse mortgage might make sense under several conditions:
- **Increased Home Value**: If your home's value has appreciated significantly since you first took out your reverse mortgage, refinancing could allow you to access more equity.

- **Lower Interest Rates:** If interest rates have dropped since you obtained your reverse mortgage, refinancing might allow you to secure a lower rate, which would slow the growth of your loan balance over time.
- **Change in Loan Terms:** Refinancing can also be useful if you want to switch from an adjustable-rate loan to a fixed-rate loan (or vice versa) to better align with your financial goals.

How HECM-to-HECM Refinancing Works

- **New Appraisal:** As with your initial reverse mortgage, refinancing starts with a new appraisal of your home. This determines how much equity is available.

- **New Loan Terms:** The lender will calculate new terms based on your current home value, interest rates, and the amount of time since your original loan was issued. The goal is to access any additional equity that has accrued or improve loan conditions.

- **Costs of Refinancing:** Keep in mind that refinancing comes with its own set of costs, including appraisal fees, closing costs, and potentially an origination fee. These costs are typically added to the new loan balance, so it's important to weigh whether refinancing is worth the added expense.

When Refinancing May Not Be Ideal

While refinancing can offer advantages, it's not always the right option for every homeowner. For example, if you haven't seen much appreciation in your home's value, or if the costs of refinancing would outweigh the benefits of securing better loan terms, it may not make financial sense. Additionally, if you're nearing the end of your time in the home or your loan balance has grown significantly, refinancing could eat into the remaining equity in your home.

2. HECM for Purchase

The HECM for Purchase program is another flexible option that allows seniors to use a reverse mortgage to buy a new home. This is ideal for homeowners who want to downsize, relocate, or move into a home that better suits their needs as they age, without taking on monthly mortgage payments.

How HECM for Purchase Works

Instead of taking out a reverse mortgage on your existing home, HECM for Purchase allows you to use a reverse mortgage to buy a new home. Here's how it works:

- Down Payment Requirement: You contribute a down payment toward the purchase price of the new home. The size of the down payment depends on your age, the value of the new home, and current interest rates. Typically, this down payment will range from 35-50% of the purchase price.

- Reverse Mortgage Covers the Rest: The reverse mortgage provides the remaining funds needed to purchase the home. You then live in the home without making monthly mortgage payments, just as you would with a traditional HECM reverse mortgage.

- No Monthly Payments: Like a traditional reverse mortgage, you don't have to make monthly payments as long as you meet the loan obligations, such as living in the home as your primary residence, paying property taxes and insurance, and maintaining the home.

Why Choose HECM for Purchase?

HECM for Purchase is an excellent option if you want to:

- Downsize: Many retirees look to move into a smaller, more manageable home as they age. HECM for Purchase allows you to do this while keeping cash available for other expenses, rather than tying up your funds in a new mortgage.

- Relocate: If you're moving closer to family or into a retirement community, HECM for Purchase can help you buy a new home without the burden of monthly mortgage payments.

- Age in Place: You might want to purchase a home that's more accessible, such as one with single-level living, wider doorways, or other modifications that make aging in place easier.

Considerations for HECM for Purchase

- Down Payment: Unlike traditional reverse mortgages, HECM for Purchase requires a substantial down payment. This means you'll need enough liquidity to cover this upfront cost.

- Home Eligibility: The home you purchase must meet FHA guidelines. This includes being your primary residence and meeting certain safety and structural standards.

3. Financial Planning with Reverse Mortgages

Whether you're considering refinancing or using a HECM for Purchase, reverse mortgages can be a powerful tool in your broader financial planning strategy. Here are a few ways to incorporate a reverse mortgage into your retirement plan:

- Supplement Retirement Income: If your retirement savings or income streams fall short of what you need, a reverse mortgage can provide you with the additional funds to cover living expenses, healthcare costs, or other financial needs. A reverse mortgage can serve as a safety net, giving you more financial security during retirement.

- Use a Line of Credit as a Safety Net: A reverse mortgage line of credit grows over time, offering a valuable tool for financial planning. By setting up a reverse mortgage line of credit early in retirement, you can create a financial buffer that you can draw from later, if needed. The line of credit's growth ensures that you have access to more funds in the future without having to take out additional loans or sell other assets.

- Protect Other Retirement Assets: For some retirees, a reverse mortgage allows them to avoid drawing down their other retirement assets too quickly. By tapping into home equity for income, you can give other investments (such as 401(k)s or IRAs) more time to grow, preserving those resources for later in life.

- Create a Legacy for Heirs: While reverse mortgages do reduce the equity in your home, proper financial planning can still allow you to leave a legacy for your heirs. By using reverse mortgage proceeds wisely—whether through a line of credit, monthly payments, or refinancing—you can potentially preserve other assets that can be passed down to your family.

Conclusion

HECM reverse mortgages offer a range of flexible options for homeowners, from refinancing to accessing more equity to purchasing a new home through the HECM for Purchase program. Understanding when and how to use these tools is essential for making the most of your home equity and ensuring that your reverse mortgage fits into your long-term financial plan. Whether you're considering refinancing to improve loan terms or using a reverse mortgage to buy a new home, careful planning can help you meet your financial goals during retirement.

In the next chapter, we will discuss the advantages and disadvantages of making payments on a reverse mortgage and how this strategy can impact your financial situation.

CHAPTER 15

Advanced Planning and Tax Considerations

Reverse mortgages can be an essential part of a broader financial strategy, particularly when used with a thoughtful approach to long-term planning and tax efficiency. While many homeowners choose not to make payments on their reverse mortgage, there can be significant benefits to doing so. Additionally, it's important to understand the tax implications of a reverse mortgage, and how you can incorporate these factors into your retirement and estate planning. In this chapter, we will explore the advantages of making payments on a reverse mortgage, the tax considerations you need to be aware of, and advanced financial planning strategies.

The Advantages of Making Payments on a Reverse Mortgage

While reverse mortgages are designed to eliminate the need for monthly mortgage payments, homeowners can choose to make voluntary payments on their loan. This option offers several strategic benefits and can be used to manage the growth of the loan balance or preserve home equity for heirs.

1. Reducing Interest Accrual

One of the key reasons to consider making payments on your reverse mortgage is to reduce the amount of interest that accrues over time. Reverse mortgages are structured so that interest is added to the loan balance, compounding over the life of the loan. By making payments toward the loan's interest, or even the principal, you can slow the growth of the loan balance and preserve more equity in your home.

- Reducing Loan Balance: Each payment you make directly reduces your outstanding loan balance, which in turn reduces the amount of interest that will accrue in the future. This is particularly beneficial in the early years of the loan when interest can accumulate more rapidly.

- Avoiding Ballooning Debt: If you are concerned about the impact of a growing loan balance on your estate or heirs, making payments can help control the size of the debt and ensure there is more equity left in the home when the loan comes due.

2. Increasing Your Financial Flexibility

Making voluntary payments on a reverse mortgage can also give you more financial flexibility later in life. If you reduce your loan balance over time, you may be able to access more equity through a HECM-to-HECM refinance (as discussed in Chapter 14). This allows you to tap into additional funds if your home's value increases or if you need more money to cover future expenses.

- Access to More Equity: By paying down the balance, you create more available equity in the home. If your financial needs change, you can refinance to increase your line of credit or change the terms of your reverse mortgage to suit your new goals.

3. Protecting Your Estate for Heirs

For homeowners who want to leave their home or other assets to heirs, making payments on a reverse mortgage can preserve more of the home's equity. Since the loan balance will be lower when the loan becomes due, there is a greater chance that your heirs will inherit the home or receive the remaining equity after the loan is repaid.

- Legacy Planning: If leaving a legacy is important to you, making payments can help ensure that your home retains its value for your heirs. This is especially valuable if you expect the home's value to appreciate over time, as it allows you to balance the loan payoff with the home's increasing equity.

Tax Implications of a Reverse Mortgage

One of the most significant advantages of reverse mortgages is that the loan proceeds are not considered taxable income. However, there are other important tax implications to consider when incorporating a reverse mortgage into your financial planning. Understanding how reverse mortgage proceeds interact with other income sources and potential deductions can help you maximize your tax efficiency.

1. Reverse Mortgage Proceeds Are Not Taxable

The money you receive from a reverse mortgage is considered a loan, not income, so it is not subject to federal income tax. This makes reverse mortgage proceeds an attractive option for retirees looking to supplement their income without increasing their taxable income.

- No Impact on Income Taxes: Since reverse mortgage proceeds aren't taxed, they can be used to cover living expenses, medical bills, or other costs without triggering an increase in income taxes.

- Social Security and Medicare: Because reverse mortgage proceeds are not taxable income, they also won't affect your eligibility for Social Security benefits or Medicare. This is a key advantage for retirees who rely on these programs and want to avoid any changes to their benefits.

2. Interest Payments May Be Deductible

If you make payments on your reverse mortgage, you may be able to deduct the interest you pay, but only under certain conditions. For the interest to be deductible, the loan must be considered acquisition debt—that is, the loan proceeds must have been used to buy, build, or substantially improve the home.

- Interest Deduction Rules: If your reverse mortgage qualifies as acquisition debt, any interest payments you make can be deducted from your federal taxes, just like with a traditional mortgage. However, the deduction only applies to the interest actually paid, not the interest that accrues on the loan if no payments are made.

- Limitations: If you don't make payments on the loan, the interest is not deductible until the loan is paid off in full, which typically happens when the home is sold. This means that your heirs may be able to deduct the interest when they settle the loan after your death, but you won't benefit from the deduction during your lifetime.

3. Impact on Medicaid and Other Benefits

While reverse mortgage proceeds do not affect Social Security or Medicare, they can potentially impact your eligibility for Medicaid and other need-based benefits. Medicaid eligibility is determined by your assets and income, so large reverse mortgage proceeds or keeping reverse mortgage funds in a bank account could disqualify you from these programs.

- Managing Medicaid Eligibility. If yuu're receiving Medicaid or other need-based benefits, it's important to carefully manage the reverse mortgage funds. Spending the proceeds promptly on qualifying expenses (such as healthcare or home repairs) can help you avoid disqualification from these programs.

- Asset Limits: Medicaid has strict limits on how much money you can keep in liquid assets. Any funds you hold from a reverse mortgage, particularly if they remain in your bank account for an extended period, could count as assets and affect your eligibility.

Advanced Financial Planning Strategies

Reverse mortgages can be powerful tools for advanced financial planning, allowing homeowners to access home equity while preserving other assets. Here are some strategies to consider when incorporating a reverse mortgage into your financial plan.

1. Delaying Social Security Benefits

Many retirees use reverse mortgage proceeds to delay taking Social Security benefits. By delaying Social Security, you can increase your monthly benefit amount by as much as 8% per year until you reach age 70. This strategy allows you to maximize your Social Security benefits later in life while using reverse mortgage funds to cover living expenses in the interim.

- Maximizing Retirement Income: This strategy is particularly beneficial for retirees who have a longer life expectancy and want to ensure they receive the maximum possible Social Security benefit.

2. Using a Reverse Mortgage Line of Credit as a Financial Buffer

If you set up a reverse mortgage line of credit, the unused portion grows over time, creating a financial buffer you can draw from later. This can be a valuable strategy for managing unexpected expenses, such as medical bills, or supplementing income during market downturns without having to sell investments at a loss.

- Flexibility in Retirement: The line of credit gives you the flexibility to handle unanticipated financial challenges while preserving your other retirement assets.

3. Coordinating Reverse Mortgage Proceeds with Other Investments

For retirees with a diverse portfolio of investments, reverse mortgage proceeds can be used to supplement income during market downturns, allowing you to avoid selling stocks, bonds, or other assets when their value is depressed.

- Protecting Investments: By tapping into your home equity, you can avoid drawing down your investment accounts during periods of market volatility, giving your portfolio time to recover and grow in value.

Conclusion

Reverse mortgages offer unique opportunities for advanced financial planning, whether you choose to make voluntary payments, leverage tax benefits, or use your loan proceeds to support other investment strategies. By understanding the advantages of making payments, the tax implications of your loan, and how to use a reverse mortgage in conjunction with other retirement assets, you can maximize the financial flexibility and security that a reverse mortgage provides.

In the next chapter, we'll explore how reverse mortgages interact with government benefits, such as Medicaid, and how to structure your finances to maintain eligibility for these programs.

CHAPTER 16

Government Benefits and Equity Impact

A reverse mortgage can be a useful financial tool for seniors, but it's important to understand how it may impact your government benefits and your home's equity over time. In this chapter, we'll explore how reverse mortgages interact with programs like Medicaid and Supplemental Security Income (SSI), how much equity you need to qualify for a reverse mortgage, and what happens to your home's equity as interest accrues over the life of the loan.

How Reverse Mortgages Impact Government Benefits

One of the main advantages of reverse mortgage proceeds is that they are not considered taxable income, which means they don't affect Social Security or Medicare benefits. However, need-based government programs like Medicaid and SSI do have specific income and asset limits that could be affected by reverse mortgage proceeds if not managed carefully.

1. Social Security and Medicare

Reverse mortgage proceeds do not impact Social Security or Medicare benefits because they are considered loan advances, not income. Since these programs are not means-tested (meaning they don't have income or asset limits), receiving reverse mortgage funds will not reduce or disqualify you from these benefits.

- **No Effect on Social Security Income:** Social Security is based on your work history and is not subject to income tests, so reverse mortgage payments won't impact your monthly benefit amount.

- **No Effect on Medicare:** Like Social Security, Medicare eligibility is not tied to income or assets, so using a reverse mortgage will not change your ability to receive Medicare coverage.

2. Medicaid and Supplemental Security Income (SSI)

Unlike Social Security and Medicare, Medicaid and SSI are means-tested programs, which means they have income and asset limits. If you're receiving reverse mortgage proceeds and don't manage them properly, you could risk losing your eligibility for these benefits.

Medicaid Eligibility and Reverse Mortgages

Medicaid has strict eligibility limits based on your assets and income. While reverse mortgage proceeds themselves are not considered income, any proceeds that you retain as cash or deposit into a bank account could be counted as assets and affect your Medicaid eligibility.

- **Asset Limits:** Medicaid typically limits your liquid assets to $2,000 or less (in most states) for a single person. If you withdraw money from a reverse mortgage and keep it in your bank account past the end of the month, it could push your assets above this limit, disqualifying you from Medicaid.

- **Spend-Down Strategy:** One way to manage this is by spending the reverse mortgage proceeds in the same month you receive them on qualifying expenses, such as healthcare costs, home maintenance, or paying off debts. This way, the money isn't counted against the asset limit.

Supplemental Security Income (SSI)

SSI benefits are also based on income and asset limits, and similar to Medicaid, any reverse mortgage proceeds that remain in your account at the end of the month could be counted as assets, which may disqualify you from receiving SSI.

- **Income and Asset Test:** SSI has both an income and an asset test, and while reverse mortgage proceeds don't count as income, they do count as assets if not spent within the month they are received.

- **How to Preserve SSI Eligibility**: Like Medicaid, you can preserve your eligibility for SSI by spending the proceeds quickly on allowed expenses, such as medical costs or home improvements, so they don't accumulate and exceed SSI's asset limits.

How Much Equity is Needed to Qualify for a Reverse Mortgage?

One of the key requirements for a reverse mortgage is having sufficient equity in your home. The amount of equity you need to qualify will vary based on factors such as your age, the appraised value of the home, and current interest rates.

Minimum Equity Requirement

Generally, you'll need to have at least 50% equity in your home to qualify for a reverse mortgage, though this can vary depending on the specifics of the loan. The more equity you have, the more you can borrow through a reverse mortgage.

- **Home Appraisal**: Before you can obtain a reverse mortgage, your home will need to be appraised to determine its current market value. This appraisal helps the lender calculate how much equity you have and how much you can borrow.

- **FHA Lending Limits**: For Home Equity Conversion Mortgages (HECMs), which are the most common type of reverse mortgage, the amount you can borrow is also subject to FHA loan limits. Even if your home is worth more than the FHA lending limit, the amount you can borrow will be capped based on those limits.

Age and Equity Access

The age of the borrower plays a key role in determining how much equity you can access through a reverse mortgage. The older you are, the more equity you'll be able to access. This is because the loan is expected to last for a shorter period, allowing you to borrow a larger percentage of your home's value.

- **Younger Borrowers (62-70)**: If you're on the younger side of the eligibility range (closer to 62), you'll likely be able to access a smaller percentage of your home's equity, since the loan is expected to accrue more interest over a longer period.

- Older Borrowers (70 and above): Older borrowers can typically access a higher percentage of their home's equity because the loan is expected to be repaid sooner, meaning the lender assumes less risk.

The Impact of Equity Reduction Over Time

One of the most important aspects of a reverse mortgage to understand is how it impacts your home's equity over time. While a reverse mortgage allows you to access your home's value, the loan balance grows over time as interest and fees are added to the loan. This can reduce the equity available for you or your heirs in the future.

How the Loan Balance Grows

With a reverse mortgage, interest and fees are added to your loan balance, which grows over time. Since you're not required to make monthly payments, the balance compounds, meaning it increases more quickly the longer you hold the loan.

- Interest Accrual: The interest on a reverse mortgage accrues based on the loan balance, and since no payments are required, this interest is added to the balance each month. Over time, the balance grows, reducing the amount of equity remaining in the home.

- Mortgage Insurance Premiums (MIP): For HECMs, there is an ongoing Mortgage Insurance Premium (MIP) of 0.5% that is added to the loan balance each year. This fee ensures that the loan is insured by the FHA, providing protections like the non-recourse feature (which ensures you or your heirs never owe more than the home's value).

Equity Reduction and Its Impact on Heirs

As the loan balance grows, the amount of equity left in the home decreases, which can reduce the amount available to your heirs if they inherit the home. However, thanks to the non-recourse feature of reverse mortgages, neither you nor your heirs will ever owe more than the home's appraised value, even if the loan balance exceeds the value of the home.

- Non-Recourse Protection: If the loan balance ends up being higher than the value of the home when the loan comes due (either due to market conditions or a long period of interest accrual), your heirs will not be responsible for the difference. The FHA insurance covers the shortfall, ensuring the lender is repaid and your heirs are not burdened with the debt.

- Equity Retention: While the loan balance grows, you can still retain some home equity if the value of the home appreciates over time. Additionally, as discussed in Chapter 15, making voluntary payments can help reduce the loan balance and preserve more equity.

Conclusion

Reverse mortgages can provide financial flexibility during retirement, but they can also impact your government benefits and the amount of home equity you retain over time. Understanding how reverse mortgage proceeds interact with programs like Medicaid and SSI is crucial for maintaining eligibility, while knowing how much equity is needed to qualify for the loan ensures you're prepared. Additionally, it's important to be aware of how interest and fees reduce your home's equity over time and how the non-recourse feature protects you and your heirs.

CHAPTER 17

Reverse Mortgage and Retirement Planning:
Strategic Timing for Maximum Benefit

For many retirees, planning for financial security involves balancing multiple income streams, including Social Security, pensions, investments, and home equity. A reverse mortgage can be a valuable part of this mix, allowing homeowners to tap into the wealth tied up in their homes. However, the key to maximizing the benefits of a reverse mortgage lies in strategic timing and careful integration with other financial assets. By working with a financial advisor, retirees can develop a holistic approach that ensures both immediate and long-term financial stability.

In this chapter, we'll explore five advanced strategies for using a reverse mortgage to enhance retirement planning, from delaying Social Security to protecting investment portfolios during market downturns.

Delaying Social Security to Maximize Benefits

One of the most effective strategies for boosting retirement income is to delay taking Social Security benefits. Every year that you delay claiming Social Security beyond your full retirement age, your monthly benefit increases by about 8%, up to age 70. A reverse mortgage can provide the income needed to cover living expenses in the interim, allowing you to delay Social Security and secure higher monthly payments for life.

How It Works:

- By using reverse mortgage proceeds to fund living expenses during early retirement, you can avoid drawing from Social Security, giving your benefit more time to grow.

- Once you reach age 70, when your Social Security payments max out, you can begin receiving the increased monthly benefit, while still having the option to access remaining reverse mortgage funds if needed.

Benefit:

This strategy provides a way to boost lifetime Social Security benefits, particularly for retirees in good health who expect to live longer and want to maximize guaranteed, inflation-adjusted income.

Coordinating Reverse Mortgage Proceeds with Investment Withdrawals

Many retirees rely on investments, such as IRAs, 401(k)s, or taxable accounts, to provide income. However, withdrawing from investments during market downturns can be damaging, as it locks in losses and reduces future growth potential. By using a reverse mortgage line of credit, retirees can avoid making withdrawals during periods of market volatility, preserving their investment portfolios for future growth.

How It Works:

- A reverse mortgage line of credit can serve as a buffer asset, providing liquidity when market conditions are unfavorable.

- In years when investments are down, retirees can draw on the reverse mortgage to cover expenses, allowing their portfolios to recover without needing to sell investments at a loss.

Benefit:

This strategy can protect the longevity of an investment portfolio, ensuring that retirees don't prematurely deplete their assets. Over time, this approach can lead to better overall financial outcomes, especially for retirees with a long retirement horizon.

Supplementing Income While Delaying Pension or Other Retirement Accounts

If you have access to a pension or other tax-deferred accounts like IRAs, you may want to delay drawing from these sources to allow them to grow. By using reverse mortgage proceeds to supplement income, retirees can defer taking pension payments or Required Minimum Distributions (RMDs) from retirement accounts, which allows those assets to appreciate over time.

How It Works:

- Use reverse mortgage proceeds to cover living expenses while deferring withdrawals from pensions, IRAs, or other retirement accounts.

- By delaying withdrawals, you can allow these assets to grow, potentially increasing the size of your future distributions and providing more flexibility later in retirement.

Benefit:

This strategy offers a way to maximize retirement assets, reduce taxable income (in the case of RMDs), and maintain financial flexibility in the later years of retirement.

Tax-Efficient Withdrawals: Using Reverse Mortgages to Manage Tax Brackets

One of the lesser-known advantages of reverse mortgage proceeds is that they are not considered taxable income. This offers a unique opportunity to manage your tax bracket, especially if you're nearing a higher income tax threshold. By using reverse mortgage funds to supplement your retirement income, you can keep your taxable withdrawals from investments lower, reducing the likelihood of moving into a higher tax bracket.

How It Works:
- Work with a financial advisor to create a tax-efficient withdrawal plan, using a combination of investment withdrawals and reverse mortgage proceeds to minimize taxable income.

- By drawing on non-taxable reverse mortgage funds, you can reduce the amount you need to withdraw from tax-deferred accounts, lowering your overall taxable income and potentially avoiding higher tax brackets.

Benefit:

This strategy allows retirees to keep more of their income by managing taxes more effectively. It's particularly beneficial for those with large tax-deferred accounts who want to reduce the tax impact of withdrawals.

Using a Reverse Mortgage to Fund Long-Term Care and Insurance Premiums

Long-term care costs can be a significant financial burden, and many retirees purchase long-term care insurance to cover potential future expenses. However, insurance premiums can be high, and some retirees may struggle to afford them. A reverse mortgage can be used to fund insurance premiums or to cover long-term care costs directly, ensuring that retirees have access to care without depleting other assets.

How It Works:
- Use reverse mortgage proceeds to pay for long-term care insurance premiums, ensuring coverage for potential future needs.

- Alternatively, use a reverse mortgage to fund in-home care or assisted living costs directly, without the need for insurance.

- A reverse mortgage line of credit can grow over time, providing a valuable safety net if long-term care expenses arise unexpectedly.

Benefit:

This strategy helps retirees manage long-term care costs without disrupting their overall financial plan or liquidating other assets. It can also provide peace of mind knowing that care needs will be met, whether through insurance or direct funding.

Conclusion

While reverse mortgages can be a powerful tool in retirement planning, they are most effective when integrated into a broader financial strategy. A financial advisor can help retirees assess their overall financial situation, determine the best timing for using a reverse mortgage, and coordinate its use with other retirement assets. By taking a strategic approach, retirees can ensure that their home equity works in tandem with other income sources, providing both immediate and long-term financial security.

CHAPTER 18

Proprietary Reverse Mortgages and Loan Servicing

In addition to the federally insured Home Equity Conversion Mortgages (HECMs), there are also proprietary reverse mortgages that may be an option for certain homeowners. These private reverse mortgages offer unique benefits and may be more suitable for homeowners with higher-value properties. This chapter will explore proprietary reverse mortgages, how they differ from HECMs, and what to expect during the loan servicing process, including how your loan is managed over time and your responsibilities as a borrower.

Proprietary Reverse Mortgages: What Are They?

A proprietary reverse mortgage is a reverse mortgage that is not insured by the Federal Housing Administration (FHA) and is instead offered by private lenders. These loans are often referred to as jumbo reverse mortgages because they are typically geared toward homeowners with high-value properties who need access to more equity than what is allowed under HECM loan limits.

How Proprietary Reverse Mortgages Work

While proprietary reverse mortgages function similarly to HECMs, with no required monthly payments and the loan being repaid when the borrower sells the home or passes away, there are key differences between the two.

- Loan Limits: Proprietary reverse mortgages are not subject to the FHA's maximum lending limits. This means that homeowners with higher-valued homes can borrow more than the amount allowed under a HECM. For example, while HECMs have a limit based on the FHA's maximum home value (currently $1,089,300 for 2024), proprietary reverse mortgages may allow you to access a larger portion of your home's equity.

- No FHA Insurance: Unlike HECMs, proprietary reverse mortgages do not come with FHA mortgage insurance. This means that there is no government guarantee protecting you or your heirs from owing more than the value of the home. However, many proprietary reverse mortgages still offer non-recourse provisions, meaning you won't owe more than the home's value at the time of repayment, though this is not always guaranteed.

- Flexibility in Eligibility: Proprietary reverse mortgages may have more flexible eligibility requirements, including less stringent age requirements (some lenders offer them to homeowners as young as 55) or property types that don't qualify under HECM rules, such as certain luxury homes or higher-priced condominiums.

When to Consider a Proprietary Reverse Mortgage

A proprietary reverse mortgage may be the right option if you:
- Own a high-value home and need access to more equity than a HECM allows.

- Have a home that doesn't qualify for a HECM because of FHA restrictions.

- Prefer the flexibility of private loan terms, such as the ability to borrow a higher percentage of your home's value.

However, it's important to weigh the pros and cons carefully, as proprietary reverse mortgages lack the consumer protections and FHA insurance associated with HECMs.

Key Differences Between HECM and Proprietary Reverse Mortgages

Understanding the differences between HECM and proprietary reverse mortgages can help you decide which option is better suited to your needs:

- Loan Limits: HECM loans are capped by FHA limits, while proprietary loans allow for larger loan amounts, especially for high-value homes.

- Insurance: HECMs come with FHA mortgage insurance, which protects both borrowers and lenders. Proprietary loans do not have this insurance but may include similar protections, such as non-recourse provisions.

- Fees and Costs: Proprietary reverse mortgages may have different fee structures compared to HECMs. For example, they may not require mortgage insurance premiums (MIP), which can reduce the overall cost of the loan. However, proprietary loans may come with higher interest rates or origination fees to compensate for the lack of government backing.

- Property Types: Certain types of properties, such as luxury homes or non-FHA-approved condominiums, may qualify for proprietary reverse mortgages but not for HECMs.

Loan Servicing: What to Expect After Closing

Once you've closed on your reverse mortgage—whether it's a HECM or a proprietary loan—the servicing process begins. This is the ongoing management of your loan by the lender or loan servicer. Loan servicing involves activities such as disbursing your loan proceeds, providing regular statements, and ensuring that you meet your obligations as a borrower.

1. Loan Proceeds Management

Depending on the payout structure you've chosen (lump sum, line of credit, or monthly payments), your loan servicer will be responsible for managing the disbursement of your loan proceeds. Here's what you can expect:

- Monthly Payments: If you've opted for a monthly payment plan, your servicer will issue these payments on a set schedule. You will receive regular statements detailing how much has been paid to you and the remaining balance.

- Line of Credit: If you've chosen a line of credit, your servicer will manage your access to those funds. You can make withdrawals as needed, and your servicer will keep track of your available credit and how it grows over time (for HECMs).

2. Monthly and Annual Statements

Your loan servicer will provide monthly or annual statements that detail important information about your loan, including:

- The current loan balance, including how much has been disbursed and how much interest has accrued.

- Any fees or charges added to the loan balance, such as servicing fees or mortgage insurance premiums.

- The remaining equity in your home (if applicable).

- These statements are important for keeping track of your loan and understanding how it is evolving over time.

3. Ongoing Responsibilities

While a reverse mortgage eliminates the need for monthly mortgage payments, you still have important responsibilities to keep the loan in good standing. These include:

- Paying Property Taxes: You must stay current on your property taxes. If you fall behind on taxes, the loan servicer may declare the loan due and payable.

- Maintaining Homeowners Insurance: Keeping homeowners insurance in place is essential to protect your home and meet the terms of the reverse mortgage. If your insurance lapses, the servicer could also call the loan due.

- Maintaining the Home: The home must be kept in good condition. If the property falls into disrepair, the loan servicer may require repairs to be made or take steps to call the loan due if the condition significantly deteriorates.

Failure to meet these obligations can result in the loan becoming due prematurely, which may lead to foreclosure if the loan balance cannot be repaid.

4. Loan Servicer Contact and Support

Your loan servicer will be your primary point of contact throughout the life of the reverse mortgage. Whether you have questions about your loan balance, payout options, or need to update your contact information, the loan servicer is responsible for managing these aspects.

- Customer Service: Loan servicers are required to provide ongoing customer service, ensuring that you understand the status of your loan and have access to all relevant information.

- Payment Changes: If your financial situation changes, or if you want to adjust your payout structure (such as switching from a line of credit to monthly payments), you'll need to contact your loan servicer to discuss your options.

5. What Happens When the Loan Becomes Due?

The loan becomes due and payable when a maturity event occurs, such as when:

- The last borrower passes away.

- The home is no longer the primary residence (for example, if the borrower moves into a nursing home).

- The borrower fails to meet ongoing obligations, such as paying property taxes or maintaining insurance.

At this point, the servicer will begin the process of settling the loan. The options typically include selling the home to repay the loan or refinancing the loan balance to keep the home. If the loan balance exceeds the home's value, the non-recourse feature of most reverse mortgages ensures that you or your heirs will not owe more than the home's current value.

Conclusion

Proprietary reverse mortgages offer an alternative for homeowners with higher-value properties who need more equity than a HECM allows. However, they come with different features, such as the absence of FHA insurance, that borrowers need to consider carefully. Once you have a reverse mortgage, the loan servicing process becomes an essential part of managing your loan and ensuring that it stays in good standing. By understanding the responsibilities and support available during servicing, you can ensure your reverse mortgage remains a valuable financial tool.

In the next chapter, we'll discuss the steps necessary to pay off a reverse mortgage and how to handle the loan when it becomes due.

CHAPTER 19

Paying Off a Reverse Mortgage
And Helpful Hints

At some point, whether due to selling the home, moving into long-term care, or passing the home to heirs, your reverse mortgage will need to be paid off. Understanding the process for repaying a reverse mortgage and knowing what to expect can help avoid confusion and ensure a smooth transition. In this chapter, we'll explore how to pay off a reverse mortgage, provide helpful tips for managing the loan effectively, and highlight red flags to watch out for throughout the life of the loan.

How to Pay Off a Reverse Mortgage

Reverse mortgages are typically repaid when a maturity event occurs. These events include the borrower's passing, the sale of the home, or the borrower moving into permanent long-term care. When the loan becomes due, the full balance—consisting of the loan principal, accrued interest, and any associated fees—must be repaid. Here's how the repayment process works.

1. When the Loan Becomes Due

A reverse mortgage becomes due and payable when one of the following occurs:
- The borrower (or last surviving co-borrower) passes away.
- The home is no longer the borrower's primary residence (for example, if the borrower moves into a nursing facility for more than 12 consecutive months).

- The borrower sells the home or moves out permanently.

- The borrower fails to meet the loan's requirements, such as maintaining the property, paying property taxes, or keeping homeowners insurance.

Once the lender is notified of the maturity event, the borrower or their heirs typically have six to twelve months to repay the loan. During this period, the home can be sold to cover the loan balance, or the loan can be repaid using other funds.

2. Selling the Home to Repay the Loan

In many cases, the easiest way to repay a reverse mortgage is by selling the home. If the home's value is higher than the loan balance, the proceeds from the sale will go toward paying off the loan, and any remaining equity will go to the homeowner or heirs.

- Appraisal and Market Value: The lender may require an appraisal to determine the home's market value. If the home is sold for more than the loan balance, the remaining equity belongs to the homeowner or their heirs.

- Non-Recourse Protection: If the loan balance exceeds the home's value, the non-recourse provision ensures that the borrower or heirs will not owe more than the appraised value of the home. The FHA insurance will cover the difference.

3. Repaying the Loan Without Selling the Home

In some cases, heirs or the borrower may want to keep the home instead of selling it. To do this, the loan must be paid off in full, which can be done by:

- Using Other Funds: The borrower or heirs can pay off the loan using savings, investments, or other assets.

- Refinancing the Loan: Heirs may choose to refinance the reverse mortgage with a traditional mortgage, particularly if they plan to keep the home.

- If the loan balance is higher than the home's value, heirs can pay off the reverse mortgage for 95% of the home's appraised value, thanks to the non-recourse provision.

4. Dealing with Interest and Fees

When the loan becomes due, the final balance will include:

- The amount initially borrowed.
- All accrued interest over the life of the loan.
- Ongoing fees, such as servicing fees or mortgage insurance premiums (for HECMs).

These amounts will be rolled into the final payoff amount. The longer the reverse mortgage is held, the more interest and fees will accrue, so it's important to understand how the loan balance grows over time.

Helpful Tips for Managing a Reverse Mortgage

Managing a reverse mortgage effectively is key to avoiding complications and ensuring that you can access your home equity without jeopardizing your financial stability. Here are some helpful tips for managing your reverse mortgage throughout its life.

1. Stay Current on Property Taxes and Insurance

Even though you don't need to make monthly mortgage payments, you are still responsible for paying property taxes, homeowners insurance, and maintaining the home. Failure to meet these obligations could cause the loan to become due prematurely.

- Tip: Set up reminders or automatic payments to stay on top of these expenses, ensuring that you don't accidentally fall behind. If you struggle with these costs, consider setting aside part of your reverse mortgage proceeds in a Life Expectancy Set-Aside (LESA), which can cover taxes and insurance.

2. Maintain Your Home

The condition of your home is critical because it serves as the collateral for your reverse mortgage. Lenders may require repairs if the home falls into disrepair, and failure to keep the home in good condition could cause the loan to become due early.

- Tip: Make a plan for regular maintenance and address any significant repairs as soon as they arise. Using reverse mortgage proceeds for necessary repairs can help ensure the home retains its value.

3. Communicate With Your Lender

Keeping an open line of communication with your loan servicer is crucial. If you have questions about your loan, receive notifications about missed obligations, or experience changes in your financial situation, contacting your lender promptly can help resolve issues before they become serious.

- Tip: Review your loan statements regularly to ensure that you understand the current balance, interest accrual, and any fees added to the loan. If anything looks unusual or confusing, don't hesitate to reach out to your lender for clarification.

4. Plan for the Future

Reverse mortgages can significantly impact your estate planning. If you want to leave your home to your heirs, communicate your intentions with them early and ensure they understand the process for paying off the loan. This can help avoid surprises later.

- Tip: Consider consulting with a financial advisor or estate planning attorney to ensure that your reverse mortgage fits into your overall financial and estate planning strategy.

Red Flags to Watch Out For

While reverse mortgages are heavily regulated, there are still potential pitfalls to be aware of. Understanding the red flags can help you avoid falling into financial traps or making decisions that could negatively impact your home equity.

1. Unsolicited Offers

Be cautious of unsolicited offers from lenders or individuals pushing reverse mortgages. Reputable lenders will never pressure you into a reverse mortgage or use scare tactics to get you to sign up.

- **Red Flag**: If someone is aggressively marketing a reverse mortgage to you without understanding your financial situation or personal goals, this is a sign of a predatory practice. Always seek out a reputable, HUD-approved lender for reverse mortgage inquiries.

2. Pressure to Invest Your Loan Proceeds

Be wary of anyone who pressures you to invest your reverse mortgage proceeds in products like annuities, stocks, or other financial vehicles. Reverse mortgages are intended to provide financial flexibility, not to be used for high-risk investments.

- **Red Flag**: If someone suggests using your reverse mortgage funds to make investments without considering your financial stability, this could be a sign of elder financial abuse.

3. Misleading Terms

Before signing any loan documents, make sure you fully understand the terms of your reverse mortgage, including interest rates, fees, and repayment conditions. If something seems unclear or too good to be true, ask questions.

- **Red Flag**: If a lender avoids explaining the details of the loan or rushes you through the process without addressing your concerns, take the time to get a second opinion or seek out counseling through a HUD-approved advisor.

Conclusion

Paying off a reverse mortgage is an important process that may involve selling your home, using other assets to repay the loan, or refinancing. By understanding how the loan is repaid and preparing for this eventuality, you can ensure a smoother experience for you or your heirs. Along the way, staying on top of your responsibilities and recognizing potential red flags will help you avoid common pitfalls and make the most of your reverse mortgage.

In the next chapter, we will cover the top consumer protections in place for reverse mortgage borrowers and how these safeguards ensure a secure and transparent lending process.

CHAPTER 20: Next Steps and Ideal Candidates

Reverse mortgages can be a valuable financial tool for the right homeowners, but they are not for everyone. This final chapter will outline who makes an ideal candidate for a reverse mortgage and provide guidance on the next steps in the process if you're considering moving forward. By understanding both the qualities of a good reverse mortgage candidate and the actions you need to take, you can determine if this option aligns with your financial goals.

Who is the Ideal Candidate for a Reverse Mortgage?

A reverse mortgage can provide financial flexibility, supplement retirement income, and help homeowners remain in their homes without the burden of monthly mortgage payments. However, it's important to consider whether a reverse mortgage is the right fit for your personal situation. Here are some factors that make someone an ideal candidate for a reverse mortgage.

1. Age and Eligibility

Reverse mortgages are designed for homeowners who are 62 years or older (some proprietary reverse mortgages have lower age requirements). The older you are, the more home equity you can typically access, making reverse mortgages more advantageous for seniors in their late 60s, 70s, or beyond.

- Why Age Matters: Since loan amounts are based in part on your life expectancy, older borrowers can usually access a larger percentage of their home's value than younger borrowers. This makes reverse mortgages particularly appealing for those nearing or in retirement who want to increase their financial resources.

2. Significant Home Equity

The ideal reverse mortgage candidate has a significant amount of equity built up in their home. The more equity you have, the more funds you can access through the reverse mortgage. Typically, you need at least 50% equity in your home, but the more you have, the greater the potential benefit.

- Why Equity Matters: Homeowners with substantial equity can receive more money through a reverse mortgage. Those with little or no equity are unlikely to benefit from this type of loan and may need to explore other options like home equity loans or downsizing.

3. Long-Term Homeowners

Reverse mortgages are best suited for homeowners who plan to remain in their homes for a long time. If you anticipate living in your home for several more years, a reverse mortgage can help you tap into your home's equity to cover expenses without the need to sell or move.

- Why Longevity Matters: Because reverse mortgages come with upfront costs, such as origination fees and mortgage insurance premiums, they make more sense for those planning to stay in their home long term. Short-term homeowners may not see the same benefits and could end up paying more in fees than they receive in loan proceeds.

4. Desire to Stay in the Home

Reverse mortgages are ideal for seniors who want to age in place and remain in their homes for as long as possible. If selling your home or moving into assisted living is not part of your immediate plans, a reverse mortgage can provide the funds you need to stay in your home comfortably.

- Why Staying Put Matters: Since reverse mortgages are repaid when you sell the home or no longer live there as your primary residence, it's important to plan to stay in the home. If you plan to sell or move soon, a reverse mortgage may not be worth the costs and could become a burden.

5. Need for Financial Flexibility

Many seniors choose a reverse mortgage to supplement their income during retirement, pay for unexpected expenses like medical bills, or make home modifications that make aging in place easier. If you're looking for a way to improve your financial situation without monthly payments, a reverse mortgage may be a good option.

- Why Financial Flexibility Matters: Reverse mortgages allow you to access your home's equity in a variety of ways—lump sum, line of credit, or monthly payments—giving you flexibility to manage your finances. Homeowners who need additional funds but want to avoid taking on debt payments can benefit from this option.

6. Comfortable with Loan Terms and Responsibilities

Finally, the ideal candidate understands the responsibilities of a reverse mortgage and is comfortable with its terms. You must continue to pay property taxes, homeowners insurance, and keep up with home maintenance. Additionally, understanding how interest and fees accrue is important for ensuring that a reverse mortgage is a good long-term decision.

- Why Understanding the Terms Matters: Borrowers who fully understand the structure and implications of a reverse mortgage—such as the impact on home equity and potential inheritance for heirs—are more likely to make informed and beneficial decisions.

Next Steps in the Reverse Mortgage Process

If you've determined that a reverse mortgage might be the right option for you, there are specific steps to follow to ensure a smooth process. Here's what you can expect as you move forward.

1. Speak with a HUD-Approved Counselor

The first step in applying for a Home Equity Conversion Mortgage (HECM), the most common type of reverse mortgage, is to participate in HUD-approved counseling. This counseling session is mandatory and helps ensure that you understand how reverse mortgages work and how they will affect your finances.

- Why Counseling Matters: Counseling ensures that you're making an informed decision and provides you with alternatives, if applicable. The counselor will review your financial situation and help determine if a reverse mortgage aligns with your goals.

2. Find a Reputable Lender

Next, you'll need to choose a lender who offers reverse mortgages. It's important to work with a reputable, HUD-approved lender to ensure that you receive the best terms and avoid potential pitfalls.

- How to Choose a Lender: Shop around and compare lenders' fees, interest rates, and loan terms. Be sure to choose a lender who is transparent about the loan's costs and willing to answer all your questions.

3. Complete the Application Process

Once you've chosen a lender, the next step is to complete the reverse mortgage application. This includes submitting necessary documents, such as proof of income, homeownership, and details about your property. Your lender will also order an appraisal of your home to determine its current value.

- Appraisal Importance: The appraisal is crucial because it determines how much equity you have and, subsequently, how much you can borrow.

4. Choose Your Payout Option

When your reverse mortgage is approved, you'll need to decide how you want to receive your loan proceeds. Depending on your needs, you can choose a lump sum, monthly payments, or set up a line of credit to draw from over time.

- How to Decide: Think carefully about your financial goals. A lump sum may be ideal for large expenses like paying off an existing mortgage, while a line of credit offers flexibility for future needs.

5. Closing the Loan

After your application is processed and your payout option is selected, it's time to close the loan. This involves signing final paperwork and covering any necessary closing costs, such as origination fees and mortgage insurance.

- Review the Terms: Before closing, carefully review all the terms to ensure you understand how the loan will be managed, when it becomes due, and your responsibilities as a borrower.

6. Managing the Loan Over Time

Once your reverse mortgage is in place, it's important to manage it effectively. Keep up with property taxes, homeowners insurance, and maintenance to avoid default. Also, review your loan statements regularly to track how much interest is accruing and how your loan balance is growing.

- Stay on Top of Responsibilities: Failing to meet your obligations can result in the loan becoming due, so make sure you're aware of what's required to keep the loan in good standing.

Conclusion

A reverse mortgage is more than just a financial product; it's a powerful tool designed to provide financial flexibility, security, and peace of mind to homeowners who've worked hard to build equity in their homes. By choosing a reverse mortgage, you're not only unlocking the value in your home but opening doors to a more comfortable retirement without the worry of monthly payments.

For those with substantial home equity who plan to stay in their homes long-term, a reverse mortgage can be the right solution to help meet various needs—whether covering healthcare costs, enhancing daily living, or simply adding a cushion to enjoy life's moments with confidence.

If you feel that a reverse mortgage might be a fit for you, please, reach out directly to me. Together, we can review your unique financial landscape and look at real, tailored figures that show how a reverse mortgage could work for you. This is a critical part of understanding how much you may benefit and ensuring this decision aligns with your goals and circumstances.

Throughout this process, you'll have my full support and transparency, as well as the resources needed to make an informed, comfortable choice. By contacting me directly, you're not only gaining a personalized analysis but also a trusted partner committed to guiding you toward financial solutions that truly support your future. This concludes our guide, but your journey toward financial flexibility and stability can begin now. Take the first step and reach out—I'm here to help you explore the possibilities and create a retirement strategy that makes the most of what you've built.

Unlocking Home Equity: The Ultimate Guide to Reverse Mortgages

South Florida REVERSE MORTGAGE

GIAN CARLO BAVARO, MBA

RESIDENTIAL MORTGAGE & REVERSE MORTGAGE SPECIALIST

📞 (954) 228-0828

✉ Gian@ReverseMortgageSouthFlorida.com

🌐 www.ReverseMortgageSouthFlorida.com

🏠 NMLS #1502605

🔊 Se Habla Español

CLEAR 2 CLOSE

Corporate NMLS# 1700825   221 W Hallandale Beach Blvd #101, Hallandale Beach, FL 33009

Printed in Great Britain
by Amazon